ANTI-CORRUPTION
COMPLIANCE
Unfiltered

ANTI-CORRUPTION
COMPLIANCE
Unfiltered

Anti-Corruption Compliance
in the Middle East

Z PRIEST

PARTRIDGE

Copyright © 2016 by Z. Priest.

Library of Congress Control Number:		2016944060
ISBN:	Softcover	978-1-4828-6623-0
	eBook	978-1-4828-6622-3

Print information available on the last page.

To order additional copies of this book, contact
Toll Free 800 101 2657 (Singapore)
Toll Free 1 800 81 7340 (Malaysia)
orders.singapore@partridgepublishing.com

www.partridgepublishing.com/singapore

Table of Contents

Warning and CMA Disclaimer

Be warned! This is not going to be everybody's cup of tea. It's rude in some places, insulting in others and not your everyday book on anti-corruption compliance – hence the word 'unfiltered'. This is a very frustrated compliance professional turned pirate, putting down on paper all of the information and thoughts she couldn't say to corporate executives, wonder-bread lawyers, VPs and managers over the past few years. Some things I couldn't say because I was trying to be professional and some because they just wouldn't listen anyway! In all fairness, if you are penis-impaired, like me, it's sometimes hard for some men to hear what you are saying over the sounds breasts make.

Some things I didn't say because swearing like a pirate and kicking people in the taint is frowned upon in the office… except in my head where it is a stress relieving, magical and soothing thing. Don't judge me! Haven't you ever been sitting patiently in meetings, appearing to be listening intently to some ego bullshit spewing out of an executive, or a wanna-be executive's mouths – wondering 'how did this person get THAT job!? Who does he have incriminating pictures of? Or just wondering why no one else can see or seems bothered that this idiot either doesn't know what he's talking about or is lying!

Admittedly, I have been told that I have a less than effective poker face and have been caught more than once with an expression of, 'are you fucking kidding me!' on my face. For the more obviously insecure of these little Caesars in these meeting, I'd have to act interested or convinced. I just threw up a little in my mouth as I wrote that because I could hardly ever manage a fake compliment – I am just not built that way. While attending such meetings there is always a very vulgar but fascinating voice in my head, the voice of my inner pirate. She would be swearing and hurling vile insults; promising to smash their pig faces into the desk, punch them in the throat or worse. The mental images of that imagined violence are what allowed me to keep a pleasant smile on my face during these bullshit group interactions. O-Ren Ishii knew exactly what to do when people start talking shit at the table.

My official CMA disclaimer: If you are easily offended by the honest expression of real life frustration, dark thoughts, explicit language, questionable grammar, vivid images of violence, sarcasm, ill-mannered sarcasm, extremely vulgar sarcasm, or any other written forms of dark humor then put this book down and go watch Fox News while you and your dog play the peanut butter game again.

However, if you can get past the crass nature of a pirate and just want some real life, usable information on anti-corruption compliance and don't mind having a laugh or five as well, then hang in there. I promise to try to include some useful information and keep my rants directed towards a higher purpose. Sometimes you just have to speak up loudly and risk offending in order to get the message across.

About speaking up… I had a male colleague who, for nearly two years had no idea what my face looked like. Every time he would talk to me he'd be staring intently at my boobs the entire time. I had tried turning slightly, crossing my arms across my chest, scarves, ducking my face down to get his eye contact, everything. Nothing got his eyes off my tits. No, this wasn't exactly sexual harassment, because I had a duty to speak up and draw the line clearly if I was made to feel it was a hostile or uncomfortable work environment. Truthfully, up to that point, I hadn't really done it. Hints don't count when it comes to speaking up. I don't think he actually even realized what he was doing, (he was a little dense), until one day I'd had enough and spoke up rather abruptly. I snatched a manila folder off my desk, held it in front of my chest and said rather coldly, "No matter how hard to stare at them, they are NOT going to talk to you." A long drawn out pause while the lights slowly came on upstairs… and his eyes slowly moved up to my face for the first time. He blushed and without a word rushed off. He would not talk or even shoot me a side-ways glance for months, but the next time he did, he was staring intently at my face with his eyes wide and unblinking. I could see it was a struggle not to look at Thelma and Louise. It was like trying not to notice a huge zit on someone's face, or focus on the 'good eye' when you're having a conversation and the struggle is real! Because it's just there! Your eyes just go there! You just can't help but keep looking at it, you know it's there!

I had new respect for him after that though. I was made to feel uncomfortable for a nearly two years. Until I stopped hinting and just spoke up. It was awkward being around each other, but the fact that I could see he made an effort to change the unwanted behavior meant a lot to me. I understood his challenge. He is a man, and there were boobs in in front of him! I would suppose if dicks were hanging closer to men's faces it might be kind of hard to NOT look as well.

Lesson learned: speaking up on sensitive issues is not always easy. But it needs to be done, and done in a way that it makes a lasting impression leading to change. Professional is always preferable – even if it is less fun. But it doesn't always work. Speaking up loudly definitely won't make you popular, but then again real pirates don't really care for congeniality points. And deep down, we're all pirates.

"Now and then we had a hope that if we lived and were good, God would permit us to be Pirates!"

~Mark Twain

"Corruption, one way or another, will make pirates of us all."

~ Z. Priest

SECTION I

Introduction

1

The Bigger Picture – Why ethics and compliance matters are bigger than all of us

In the beginning there was chaos… and then the cavemen came.. put on suites and became executives. While it tempting to engage in overkill and go into the history of how societies developed laws for the good of all, I won't do that. That is text book on Criminology, which is definitely an acquired taste. The short version is that there are rules! Surprise! These rules are supposed to apply to everyone! Rules are put into place, revised, developed and given life with the overall goal in protecting us as a society and as individuals. Yes, in that order! In the eternal wisdom of Dr. Spock, the needs of the many out weight the needs of the one. Laws are either criminal or civil; criminal laws are in place to protect society, not the individual – even though it may be an individual who was the victim. The basic idea behind a criminal law is that an action is made criminal because if the action became the normal practice, society would crumble – Hell would freeze over, Sharia law be implemented only in the southern parts of the United States, Fox News would actually report news and the end would be upon us.

Civil law is, at its most basic, a way to discourage and punish disruptive behavior, governs how we interact with each other, and allow us to recover from those who do us wrong and cost us pain, suffering and money.

Anti-corruption laws can be both criminal and civil. They are meant to protect the greater good of all, and provide a means for individuals to recover

1

damages. They are in place to try to force corporations and individual in those corporations to play fair, keep business clean and on an even playing field for all. Corporations implement ethics and compliance programs in an attempt to either self-govern or just make themselves look good; while attempting to protect the company, its shareholders and executives from behavior that would cost them in fines, put someone in prison or both. While Compliance Programs are greatly about adherence to law, the programs themselves are *a behavioral science matter.* This is one of my pet peeves when talking with members of management. They have this preconceived idea that compliance belongs either to law or internal auditing. Compliance professionals are either all about finance and auditing or they have to be lawyers. They stubbornly cling to outdated and narrow minded views of what compliance used to be. Compliance is more now days! It is about implementing polices, practices, training and awareness which are meant to change, influence, guide and standardize *the behavior* of individuals in a company to act and conduct the business of the company in a way to keep them their asses out of trouble, out of the news and out of the courtrooms. Basically, to 'B. F. Skinner' people into doing the right thing.

When a company does get caught in a violation, they can get horribly large criminal and civil fines for not having taken the necessary precautions and implementing a compliance program. Weatherford paid USD $250 million to settle claims with the US Security Exchange Commission ("SEC") and the Department of Justice ("DOJ") for failure to establish internal controls (that's a compliance program for executives who still think they get it, but really don't) and to prevent FCPA violations. Wow, what a waste. Listen if executives don't mind throwing out that much money on something that was completely avoidable, why do you throw such bitch fits about giving employees raises or benefits? Oh that's right, I forgot for a second. It's ok to waste the company's fixing your fuck ups, but not investing in your human resources. It's the same thing as it being OK to spend millions rebuilding the warehouse and replacing its content after it's been half burned down in a fire; because it has to be done. But when it was time to invest in a good fire detection and prevention system, there were budget restrictions. Fuck ups. Entirely preventable, fuck ups.

2

What, Where, and Who in a Compliance Program

Some of the first questions companies have in deciding to implement a compliance program are:

- **What** exactly does a compliance program consist of?
- **Where** in the organization should it go?
- **Who** is supposed to be in charge?

Most companies already have some compliance components in place, so they aren't completely new to the subject. But sometimes the fact that they know *a little* about compliance gives them a false sense of security in believing they completely understand what a compliance program is. Any doctor, lawyer, audit or compliance professional will agree, a little knowledge is a dangerous thing. I wish I had a dollar for every time I've heard an executive say, "Oh, we already have compliance in our company. Finance has its own, Auditing, and HR has its own… each department handles its own compliance." Every time I hear this dumbass statement coming out of an executive's mouth I just want to knock him down, take his wallet and kick him in the nuts for just for fun! And why the hell shouldn't I?! He's letting everyone else do it.

Imagine you owned a fruit orchard. You pay people by the kilogram to pick the fruit. At the end of the day, each person tells you how many kilos they picked. You don't weigh them yourself; you just take their word for it. How long are you going to stay in business? Not fucking long! The same executives who allow organizations to self-regulate will also brag about how much his or her people love them. Of course they do! You don't hold them accountable for anything! You can't because you have no fucking clue what they may or may not be doing! Although I am sure you *think* you do and would argue vehemently that you are aware of everything that happens in your organization! But the truth is, you can't even reward them for doing well, because you can't measure or track that either! You're like those 'cool' parents who want to be 'friends' with their kids. So they allow boy/girl sleep overs and drinking... but only as long as they are in the house and not running out in the streets where all the really bad stuff happens, and they think it's safe in the house! Those same 'cool' parents are genuinely shocked when someone ends up pregnant or in the emergency room with alcohol poisoning. Everyone saw that shit coming, except them! If you're *that* kind of executive... you deserve to have your ass handed to you for your arrogance and any half-way decent pirate could just sail away with your fucking ship, leaving you flabbergasted while bobbing up and down in the water. The last time I heard this bullshit coming out of an executive's mouth I wanted to yell, "Organizations do not self-regulate on compliance dumbass! Not ever! And you better be fucking careful about repeating that same ignorant shit in front of someone you're actually trying to impress. Because if they have half a brain and any idea about governance and compliance controls, they'll see right through you and see you're a fucking idiot stepping off the short bus of management. The bus ain't short because it's exclusive!" Let's get down to it then!

WHAT: The first mystery of compliance; what exactly is a Compliance Program? First, it isn't always called 'compliance program'. It can be an enterprise risk management system, an ethics & compliance program, anti-corruption programs, etc. There is never a 'one size fits' all program. Like I mentioned, a compliance program is a lot like a fire protection system which is designed to prevent, detect and put out fires. It is a system of policies, practices and procedures which will allow for the prevention, detection and early response to issues of poor ethics or illegal behavior in the company. Issues that could cost the company good employees, good clients, embarrassing press coverage which destroys its reputation and may cause stock prices to go down, criminal and civil fines and in some cases can result in executives and board members going to prison, not to mention sometimes in high risk industries

– shit blows up for real and people die. As a corporate compliance professional, I have to admit – I truly want to prevent the company's loss of good employees, bad press, litigation, fines and of course death and destruction. The only thing I honestly would not lose sleep over is if a few executives were to go to jail. My interest is the company; companies add value to the market place and economy – not the bad management which run them into the ground. If management doesn't value compliance, or was misbehaving and putting the company at risk, then law enforcement would be doing the company a favor making them go away. Maybe it would set a good example for the next executive; 'manage your shit better or you to can take showers with a large sweaty man named Bubba in prison who admires your tight end!' They should make soap on a rope in the shape of a business card for white collar criminals, 'Bendover, Inc.' Job Title: White Knuckled Ankle Grabber. You won't be the VP or CEO in here baby! You're just Bubba's bitch! Hapy Thawts!

I will go into details about the various components that make up an outstanding Compliance Program, and what affect it will have on the enterprise if some bonehead makes the summary decision about excluding them.

WHERE: Another question is where to put a Compliance organization in the company's organization chart. You will get different answers depending on whom you ask. This decision can end up in a crippling turf war between organizations that want it under their own umbrella. Some will wage all out warfare to prevent another organization's compliance oversight on them. I am aware of one company having suffered such a nasty turf war between Auditing and Law that the executive management just stuck it under HR to resolve it. An incredible wasted effort because it's HR, so they took 'compliance' out of the organization altogether leaving it as just a corporate ethics organization. They have no authority, no reporting, and no support from any other organization. Two years in and it still had not published a decent Code of Conduct or developed an anonymous reporting mechanism. They could have licensed one, LIKE EVERYONE ELSE, but they decided to be self-aggrandizing boneheads and 'build their own from scratch' to show their worth. Waste of time and money. Licensing this software is about US$7,000.00 a year and takes about 2 to 4 months for implementation. Designing a software application so far out of the company's normal wheel house and unfamiliar from scratch can cost an IT organization hundreds of thousands of dollars and take anywhere from a year to failing to get it done at all. Idiot moves, all of it! Fuck ups. This company's 'Ethics' group meets with different department's management and shares warm, fuzzy feelings about ethics and have absolutely no teeth to enforce a damn thing. The whole effort seems equivalent to giving out puppies to spoiled children. They will be played with for a while and then ignored.

Turf wars on who will be watching whom can get really ugly and end up with the entire company suffering. When organizations in a company are so tangled up in a tug-of-war over who will own the compliance program administration – to the point that they would allow a stalemate and end of up with an HR run organization managed by the Care Bears, then I seriously question whether the motivation was to have an actual compliance program or just a power play. What's really absurd is when an HR organization actually tries to own ethics and compliance programs. It's like having a six year old insist they can bake a cake all by themselves. They get the general idea of how to do it because they've seen mommy do it before. It's cute that they want to do it, but do you actually want them try to work with the oven or the electric mixer. Plus, to be honest, most compliance violations happen in HR or labor relations anyway. Fox guarding the hen house. Fuck up!

So where are you supposed to put it? **Best case scenario**: if you want the compliance program to be strong, you need to keep it as independent and yet protected as possible; close to the top brass (General Counsel, General Auditor, CEO and Board). The compliance organization needs to be supported by every other organization in the company. (I'll explain how on that later.) Your compliance professionals need to be protected from retaliation and given the authority to do their job! That means reporting to the board, not management! That organization is the executive management and board's eyes and ears into the corporation, the thermometer for the health of the organization; lessening the chance of filtered information, dishonesty and dumbasses. A board that keeps that compliance program independent and protected will get more real-time information about the company, and be able to make better informed decisions. They'll be able to respond faster, more consistently and effectively to issues before they're big problems. The only way this can be set up is if the board makes the decision to set this up, use it, support and protect it, and accept that it will change the course of actions they're used to taking but it will allow them to be better at managing the company. Think of it as installing

CCTV all over your house – so even when you're out of town, you can just go to your security page, log in and see what's going on all over the entire company without your kids ever knowing you're watching. Better yet, they know and they behave in your house because you'll kick their ass if they don't. (*Note to self: go to Radio Shack*)

Sad truth is that a lot of directors don't really give a rat's ass about compliance. They're just happy to have the title of Board Member displayed on LinkedIn, the free travel and expensive hotels, treated like little kings sitting in thrones too big for their flabby asses, seeing their pictures in the company's press releases which they frame for their office. If you happen to be sitting on a board, and take offense at my opinion of some directors, take a look around your own office. (This goes for management to.) Count how many pictures you have of you with other important people, plaques or awards with your name on it – accompanied by a picture of when you received it. Then go home and count how many pictures of you are on the wall in your family's living room. If there are more pictures of you in your own office than your family has of you in the living room, well then I guess you matter most to YOU! And truthfully, it's ok to be proud of your accomplishments, really. Your company and your employees only ask that you do something with that power for others as well. Use your power for good and not self-serving purposes. No jokes here. If God blessed you with a position of authority and you fail to leave the organization better than when you found it, then you are useless and have wasted everyone's time. You're not one of the good guys! No matter what your wife, kids or mistresses say! You're the kind of management that causes people to leave a company. You're the one everyone complains about. Remember those VPs and executives that everyone scrambled to cozy up to because they were so powerful when you were coming up through the ranks? Then after retirement they just disappeared? That's because once they were no longer sitting in those little corporate thrones, no one gave a shit about them. They cease to be relevant to anyone, because they failed to make a positive difference when they had the chance. Their families had already moved on to living a life without them because they gave so much to the job and ignored family. The people they worked with and managed are glad they left, and no one seeks their time or attention now. They added no value, and therefore have no value. Corporations are like bathrooms - in that you should always leave it in better condition than when you found it. If you can do that, may God bless you a thousand times over for every employee whose life and circumstances you made better because you did a good job. And, likewise, may God make you feel all of the pain and suffering of those whom you COULD have helped but didn't; and ten times the pain of all the people you stepped on to get where you are. *Karma's a bitch!* If you were one of those executives who made promises to employees to get their continued best efforts and then didn't give them what you promised, or even what was in their contract… and got away with it… your day will come. Every nasty, faithless, little bug-fucker who only feels 'big' standing on the necks of others will eventually get their comeuppance!

There are directors and executives who do actually care and recognize the value of a real compliance program. They know and *most importantly* readily admit they are not experts on compliance issues. These rare executives are smart enough to know they need to have experts manage the issue for them. Then there are those who recognize the need but aren't strong enough to speak up and insist on anything; too scared to be the first to bring up something new. They wait for someone else to go first and then maybe they'll support it if it isn't too risky.

One particularly bullying director had spent the majority of a board meeting droning on and on with his words of wisdom on how things *should be done*, all based on his four years of experience as a Chairman. But he still couldn't understand that having a Compliance Committee made up of managers and VPs – and no legal, compliance or audit professionals, who met a couple times a year is *not the same* as an actual compliance program. There were other directors who knew he was full of shit, but they stayed silent because he was so overbearing – they stayed quiet; sheep. Seven out of eight directors knew that this guy was a bonehead but they stayed quiet because he was a bully… and the Chairman. Damn! Silence is more damaging than you'd think.

If all or some aspects of a compliance program are not mandated by regulation, the decision to implement a compliance organization is usually left to executive management or boards. Some will put it before a management team or committee for discussion and it will get nowhere fast. Anytime you want to spin your wheels and grind a process to a halt, put it before an unqualified committee made of people who have no background in the subject matter.

If you ask the lawyers, they'll tell you compliance is a legal issue and should be under the legal department's umbrella. If you ask auditing, they'll tell you it's an area of auditing and it should be under them. Human Resources will claim that because it has to do with investigations into employees, policies and training it belongs to them. And the correct answer is… (*drum roll please*) they are all right. Confused? While each organization plays a vital role in the compliance program, it does not belong exclusively to any of them. While I stand by the need for an independent compliance organization, I have seen those reporting to the General Counsel or General Auditor or directly to the board most effective. Chief Compliance Officers will need the buy-in, support and participation of organizations across the enterprise. I suggest this to be accomplished with a **trained** Corporate Compliance Committee with representation from Law, Auditing, HR, Finance, etc. I will give more details on that later. Fully independent compliance organizations don't always get the backing and buy-in from all management. They are put at risk and I think maybe due to the mind set of some compliance professionals, we can tend to fall a more on the side of "Chicken Little" when it comes to our concerns. Our mind-set is law and compliance, but more of a criminal law, law enforcement mind set. When the Chief Compliance Officer (CCO) reports to the General Counsel (GC), it can be a good match *if the General Counsel understands compliance programs isn't strictly about law.* It is a behavioral science and they need to just step back, listen to what the Chief Compliance Officer has to say and offer. Also, as long as the CCO doesn't get overly sensitive from having someone else supervising their kitchen, things should be relatively harmonious. The CCO must understand the value of having a supportive GC or General Auditor (GA) who recognizes and values their contribution in relation to administering the compliance program, is willing to be the one to supervise and fall on their sword if necessary. It is a good match, the CCO ying to their (GC or GA) yang. A healthy balance between what a compliance professional wants to do, and what the general counsel and general auditors says they can do.

Ultimately, where to place a compliance organization in the company is a business decision that will have to be made considering how strong your commitment to the directive is. The higher up and the more independent the organization, with board and CEO support, the more effective it can be.

WHO: Once you figure out the 'Where', the 'Who' isn't that hard to get to. Lawyers may tell you the compliance organization needs to be headed up by a Chief/Corporate Compliance Officer ("CCO") with a Juris Doctorate. The compliance organizations in the US are usually under the General Counsel because they are trying to protect internal investigations from discovery processes under the Attorney/Client privilege. Also, some lawyers, mostly wonder-bread lawyers, think that if you don't have a JD, you're just not smart enough to be allowed in the room much less administering a compliance program.

The General Auditor will tell you it needs to be someone who is a Certified Fraud Examiner with a background in finance and auditing. HR, well, when it comes to compliance matters, HR is usually still trying to crack eggs without getting the shells in the bowl for cake. If most HR organizations could run the compliance program, they'd probably opt for a business analyst to run it. What could be worse than that?! I know! A company using a Mechanical Engineer whose only compliance experience was with companies who had long records of criminal corruption violations. Yes, that would be worse, and I've actually seen that happen. Law, Auditing, HR all have valid positions. They are all supposed to be involved. But they tend to be so tied to their own business line way of thinking, they miss the biggest point, and each lacks the necessary SME's to cover the other organizations' roles. ***Compliance is a behavioral science,*** with the inclusion of law, audit, finance, security, quality assurance or HR. It is all of them. Let me say that again…... ***COMPLIANCE IS A CROSS ENTERPRISE BEHAVIORAL SCIENCE***. Maybe if I say it a couple of hundred times, it will sink in.

Look at the definition of the word.

Compliance; noun

1. ***the act*** *of conforming, acquiescing, or yielding.*
2. *a tendency **to yield** readily to others, especially in a weak and subservient way.*
3. ***conformity****; accordance: in compliance with orders.*
4. ***cooperation or obedience****: Compliance with the law is expected of all.*

Compliance comes from the root, comply [kuh m-plahy] /kəm'plaɪ/ . It's a verb (used without object), complied, complying; "to act *(Get that? To ACT!)* or be in accordance with wishes, requests, demands, requirements, conditions, etc.; agree (sometimes followed by *with*): *They asked him to leave and he complied. She has complied with the requirements."*

Originating from the Italian *complire*, Spanish *cumplir* (see <u>compliment</u>) to fulfill, accomplish, and the Latin *complēre*, equivalent to *com-* <u>com-</u> + *plē-* <u>fill</u> + *-re* infinitive suffix. *Synonyms are to* acquiesce, yield, conform, obey, consent, and assent. *Antonyms are to* **refuse** or resist.

Looking at the definition of the word 'Compliance', it isn't about monitoring as in an audit role. It isn't about legal dos and don'ts as an attorney's role. It isn't about career development or managing personnel matters of employees as an HR role. It is all of those things tied up in human behavior. It is about guiding and setting expectations of business compliance and anticorruption behaviors – establishing corporate policies and practices to teach, detect, monitor, investigate, respond, analyze and report on non-compliance matters within the company. A compliance officer isn't the beginning and end of the compliance program either. They are to act as the coordinator, the program administrator and manager for a corporate compliance program; coordinating with various Subject Matter Experts ("SME's") throughout the company to ensure that all of the right people are involved at all of the right points and the program is up to date and effective.

My happy place in this would be if all of the SME's from across the enterprise synchronizing under the coordination of the Compliance Officer to run the compliance program carefully, in a balanced manner and geared towards changing and guiding the corporate behavior towards healthy compliance. That is ideal.

The head of your compliance organization should be someone with a unique balance of law, auditing, psychology and sociology, HR and management training. This person has to be mindful of the details of the trees *and the overall well-being of the forest.* They should be very approachable, assertive, and able to communicate effectively and easily with all levels of employees from janitors to board members. This individual should have planning and strategy skills. They should be able to find a needle in a haystack when conducting investigations, data mining in general ledgers or doing legal research. They should speak legalese to be able to communicate with lawyers to be able to translate that to normal people; the language of auditors and finance people, and HR people, and the language of Mordor to communicate with management. For international companies, they should be very fluent English speakers and have a firm grasp of the local languages as well as the religious and cultural nuances that are prevalent in the area. This person should also be an amazing trainer; capable of preparing the training materials and presenting them to every level in the company and captivating an audience's attention. Compliance can be a horribly dry topic to everyone except compliance or compliance related professionals. Also, the majority of anti-corruption compliance is produced and geared towards western countries. They may not be the best fit for other regions around the globe. So the Compliance Officer needs to be able to take into consideration the language and culture of the region they're in to be able to create training materials from scratch if need be. Off the shelf compliance training material will get a nod from management, a few minutes of the employees' time and attention, then be checked off as 'done' and forgotten about. Presenting training that is un-relatable to the area you're in, will be counterproductive. Your employees will not be able to relate what they're seeing and hearing to their daily work in your company. The result will be a mental checking out.

The training has to be engaging to keep their interest and allow them to walk away with knowledge of compliance they didn't have an hour before the training. They should be informative, have a positive attitude and be able raise awareness, instruct on correct behavior, warn and clarify consequences for bad behavior, and engage their audiences into buying in on the program. I haven't seen too many Lawyers and Auditors who excel at this part. They speak their own languages and are usually good for putting people to sleep. Your CCO should also be able to put away the smiles and get really serious, really intense, really fast when necessary to stand up to a challenge. The CCO should be someone who cannot easily be bullied, and won't back down from their principals and the training's message – but knows when it's time to get the higher powers in the pictures to kick some ass.

For more examples of effective compliance programs, look at the companies named annually as the world's most ethical companies by Ethisphere at <u>www. ethisphere.com.</u>

Two other sources for compliance programs are *The Resource Guide to the U.S. Foreign Corrupt Practices Act* and the *UK Bribery Act 2010 Guidance.* Each guide is good, together they are best. Meet both standards and you've got a top notch compliance program. It all depends on how good you want your program to be? Do you want it to be just enough to check off a box and say you have one? Or do you really want a program to set a standard you can brag about, publicize, and use to attract the best employees and clients as well as reduce your attrition rates?

The other 'Who' we need to address is the 'who needs it'? A compliance program I mean. Who needs a compliance program?

Well, every company should have one. But the size of your company, the complexity, the industry and risks of your specific company determine the complexity of your compliance program. A good guide for who needs an FCPA or UK BA compliant program would be as follows:

This is not an exhaustive list. If your company checks ANY of the categories, you need to take a closer look at what liabilities, risks and jurisdictions you may actually fall under.	US Foreign Corrupt Practices Act **DOJ & SEC**	UK Bribery Act **Serious Fraud Office**
Are you a US Company Subsidiary, Affiliate or Franchise?	X	
Are you a UK Company Subsidiary, Affiliate or Franchise?		X
Are you a joint venture of a US Company?	X	
Are you a joint venture of a UK Company?		X
Are you a distributor or agent of a US Company?	X	
Are you a distributor or agent of a UK Company?		X
Are you a public company registered with the US stock exchange?	X	

Do you have any transactions through US banks?	X	
Do you ever use US internet servers for business communications, or personal reasons but using company hardware? (mobiles, laptops or office PC)	X	
Do you have contracts in US dollars?	X	
Do you have any transactions through UK banks?		X
Do you ever use UK internet servers for business communications, or personal reasons but using company hardware? (mobiles, laptops or office PC)		X
Do you employ any UK Citizens?		X

3

Raise your hand if you don't want a Compliance Program! Dumbass

Asking 'Who doesn't want a Compliance Program' is like asking 'who hates their mother'? No one is going to actually speak up and say 'Me! My mother was a bitch!" – Even if she actually was. So who wouldn't want a real compliance program in their company??? It protects the board and the executives, gives them greater control, and provides transparency. It adds value to your business practices in that it creates greater clarity and integrity to the company for your clients, business partners, shareholders, and employees. So why would anyone not want a compliance program? In my opinion, there are three categories of people who don't want a compliance program in their company; the '**Egos**', the '**Mini-Kings**', and the '**Swans**'.

The **Egos** are those who don't understand what a compliance program actually is (and either won't admit or don't know that they don't know) or recognize the value are going to be the easiest of the three to deal with. But they are convinced they know it all and if you try to point out their shortcomings on information in the matter, you'll lose them for good. They are like mouthy, know-it-all teenagers, not really suited for the chair they're sitting in, but damn sure they deserve it more than anyone else because of their great intelligence and business skills – which they probably don't actually have. *They are delusional.* They are the ones who believe every organization can manage their own individual compliance program. They may have gotten the job through nepotism or they have naked pictures of someone they're holding for ransom. Everyone in the company usually hates them and thinks they are either evil geniuses or just really fucking arrogant and stupid. They are a liability for the company for sure. You may try to carefully 'educate them' but you need to do so in a way that they aren't made to feel dumb and *are able to save face*. You will have to be a bit of a sycophant to do this. Convince them that this program is the shit and it was all their great idea! They can be brought around. Come at them from a point of pain relief sometimes and as a way they will be able to showcase their own amazing managerial skills. Step carefully with these kids; pick your words and vocabulary carefully. Talk over their heads they'll feel intimidated and you're out. Talk down to them they feel 'lectured' or scolded or looked down on, and you're out. They will try to schmooze or bully those who intimidate them. Get them comfortable, relaxed, figure out what their level of understanding is and stay there when communicating. They are almost always guarded with new people because they work hard to keep up the persona of the 'expert in all things'. If you fail to sell the compliance program idea to them, they'll shut you out – and the company will continue to suffer because you couldn't convince them to grow up and admit they don't know it all. If you figure out how to manage all of that successfully, write me and tell me how you did it. I could never keep my poker face and bull-shit up long enough to accomplish this.

The **Mini-Kings**, are just that; kings (or queens) of their own little kingdoms. The idea of telling them you want to put a system in place that would enforce transparency and accountability will be as welcome as a turd in their birthday cereal bowl. They are not having it, and you just became a threat on their radar. Their organizations will most likely be suffering from *Authoritarian hierarchalization.* This is a dangerous strain of thought propagated within an organization by its management. The management of such an organization is in the position to make decisions having major consequences upon all of their subordinates without reproach, little or no mechanism for accountability. Whether they do or do not make such decisions is less important than the fact that they occupy such pivotal positions: their failure to act, their failure to make decisions, is itself an act that is often of greater consequence than the decisions they do make. They are in command of the major hierarchies and organizations of the company. They are enabled by (over the top) policy or lack of policy to run the machinery of the company and claim its privileges unchallenged – as they see fit. They are not willing or capable of introspection; they don't stop to question the morality or legality of their actions. They are convinced they know better than anyone. Just shut-up and do what I say mentality. And they don't give a flying fuck what anyone else thinks. I have a weird observation. Almost every Mini-King I've encountered seems to have a thing about expensive, colorful socks. Strange, I don't get it, but I've seen it.

An organization run by AH is highly vulnerable to labor abuses and wide spread ethical and compliance violations. Individuals in authority may promote AH, often without realizing what they are doing. They feel justified and right in their behavior because they are certain they are the only ones who know what is best for the company. They are the ones who will talk about 'Best Practices' but never actually implement them because it puts in too many checks and balances for their taste. Plus, many couldn't identify best practices if it had a neon sign above it. They've got lots of pictures of themselves in their offices, usually with big wigs, powerful people or celebrities. They rely solely on their own moral gauges and understanding of regulations. The effects Mini-Kings have on the organization are slow to appear at first, but eventually snow ball out of control to a point where a complete overhaul of management and policy will be required to set things right. Depending on the size and growth rate of the organization, the lag time in seeing the eventual effects can be months or even years if there are no measures in place to test the health of an organization.

These Mini-Kings *are not always the corporate officers.* If you have a weak CEO, it can be a manipulative VP or manager, or even the Assistant. They run interference with everyone in the company, working to control who sees, speaks, or has anything to contribute to the executive management team or the board. Dirty office politics is their strongest skill. They are masters at filtering and directing (or misdirecting) information, becoming the conduit of control or access to the executive management team or other decision makers either through hierarchy or influence. They are the evil advisors to the emperor who keeps the emperor ignorant and under control – Gríma Wormtongue's every one of them! They may be smiling but in reality are paranoid, often very dangerous – to you, the company and even to themselves. Some of these Mini-Kings will exhibit signs of narcissistic personality disorder and should have been on medication. And I ain't even joking about that part. Hand to the Almighty; some of these fuckers are bat shit crazy. They rarely recognize or value the expertise of others *except* in how they may utilize them for their own purpose. That is your hook, maybe your only hook. That is how you convince Mini-Kings to implement a compliance program. You need to sell the idea of a compliance program as a way for them to 'control the kingdom better, reducing their own risk' (they don't actually think they have risk, but if you can convince them they're not actually bullet proof, more power to ya!) and protecting them from enemies. Yes, you're actually kissing ass, but think of it as a small sacrifice for the greater good. Sam stuck by Frodo when he took the ring to Mordor; you can work to appeal to the 'Kiss the Ring' mentality of these little Kings. Be warned, just like Sam, the closer to get to the evil, the less others will trust your motives or even like you. You may end up being permanently linked with the Mini-King and labeled a lowly henchman. Just saying. Think of the suffering masses in their organizations. Personally, I have such strong feelings of disgust towards Mini-Kings; I have not found a way to overcome it enough to pull this off. I'd rather just let my inner pirate take over and sink my fingers into their throat. Pirates and kings don't get along, ever!

The **Swans** are against you from the beginning. No Swan will ever be in line with any compliance professional. They have too much to lose to take the chance of letting you in the door. *But they will never show you their real face.* They may openly support compliance in meetings but will carefully sabotage it behind the scenes. You will not see this one coming. Because they are already guilty of a lot of shit; taking bribes, discriminating, lying, cheating, you name it. They are rotten; they know it and they will go to great lengths to ensure no one else ever finds out. They are literally the trusted criminals in the organization. Their management thinks they are great and reliable. They micro-manage specific aspects of their organizations – but seem to let others run amok. They are often liked and admired by their peers, coming across as 'good' and involved. If you don't know anything about swans, let me enlighten you. They were once small, ugly and powerless, and they're determined never to be that again. They worked hard to become beautiful, graceful and the masters of their environment. But swans are assholes! Ask any avid golfer. They are aggressive, will attack without warning and hurt you. In my experience, it is best to try to stay below their radar – not always possible but try. The trick with Swans is that they're hard to spot. So my rule of thumb, if any executive or board member or manager seems too good to be true, they are! It could be a swan and I'd recommend keeping your eyes and ears open to know for sure. Word your compliance proposals and materials to be as benign and unthreatening language as possible – without giving up its teeth. Put the poison in the honey. Keep the sharpest teeth hidden behind the calmest, sweetest smile as long as you can. This is not meant to convince the Swan, cause you're not going to. They'll see you coming a mile away. And they are smart. This honey coated approach is meant to win over everyone else; making it as difficult as possible for the Swan to reject without exposing themselves. Be warned, once the compliance program is laid out, the one proposing it will immediately be on the Swan's hit list as the next target. They recognize hidden teeth better and faster than anyone else – they practically invented hidden teeth. They are very intelligent. They will say or do anything to destroy the credibility of an enemy and eliminate the threat of exposure. Your reputation will take some hits. They won't do it out in the open. It will all be done behind closed doors. You won't see it coming. Never try to face off with them directly; they will mostly likely outrank you. Deflect negative questions or inferences with a smile and professionally phrased answer focusing on the positive and look at everyone else in the room. Show such a positive and likable manner, with so many rainbows and sunshine shooting out your fucking ass – they'll change your name to fuck'in 'Rainbow Bright'. And, this is the most difficult part. It's got to be real. So real, that when the Swan goes after you behind closed doors, they will look suspicious for attacking such a kind and wonderful person. Find a champion who outranks them, and hide behind them like a big fat coward. If you start to hate yourself for being such a pussy, just remind yourself that it is for the good of the many. Consider it a temporary sacrifice of your dignity and identity as a "Warrior against corruption', for the betterment of the company in the long term. It won't always work, but it is always worth the effort.

You'll have your day in the sun when the compliance program is approved, developed, implemented and launched and the training starts. Because those bad apples will be exposed, they will be reported on and you can be assured that with patience the truth will come out. Shit comes out in the wash. You're challenge is to stay alive, stay strong, and out of harm's way long enough to see the program bear fruit.

SECTION II

Putting It All Together

4

Codes of Conduct

There are two kinds of company Codes of Conduct; one for the corporate section which can also be referred to as the Code of Ethics or Code of Business Standards, it is up the company. The second code is the Supplier's Code of Conduct. These two Codes are written in a similar fashion, but serve different purposes. A list of bulleted 'Company Values' is NOT a code.

The Codes is the stated commitment of the behavioral expectations that an organization holds for its employees and agents. The Codes are not the same as a compliance policy. It is not detailed enough and lacks the necessary information to be considered a policy. I will go over the policy later on. Most companies have a Code of Conduct, and to those which don't.. *"Hell'er! It is the twenty-first century! Are you planning to arrive soon?"* Codes are now common place for most corporations, and are usually shared not only with employees, but with customers and the public at large as well. However, not all Codes are created equally. Some Codes are better than others. And some Codes... just plain suck. To be successful, a Code must be believable by all stakeholders to which it applies. It must show the corporation's commitment in action has significant impact. How the Code itself is written, what it includes as well as leaves out, who is clearly designated to administer the code, and how it is communicated all play instrumental underlying roles in whether it has the power to influence not only the perceptions of its audiences, but also their actions. Keep the ten points below in mind when developing your Codes:

1. Your Code needs to be easily **available to the public**. Most companies opt to put it on the company's website and downloadable. For employees there should be a printed handy-sized copy on every desk top, and given to every new employee during their orientation and on-boarding process. In sight, in mind. It should clearly indicate what organization in the company is responsible for administering the Code, updating it and managing the reporting hotline and functions – your compliance organization! Having a good code available to the public tells a lot about your corporate culture. Not having one tells more.

2. The Codes need to convey a strong **Tone from the Top**. Your management needs to show a great deal of leadership by example and use the Code on a regular basis in discussions. Having a likable picture (not a stiff, uptight picture with an *'I got gas'* expression on their face) and message from the CEO, maybe even a group photo of the CEO with the management next to the solo picture may encourage their buy in and support. Ultimately you need to find a way to show the high level of visible commitment to the values and topics covered by the Code. Best code picture I ever say was for a small US company of about 150 employees. They took a picture all together with the management on a football field with the clause, "WE'RE IN THIS TOGETHER". And everyone was smiling!

3. The **readability** of the Code is vital. If it is too long, NO ONE WILL READ IT. It isn't 50 Shades of Gray; it is a Code of Conduct! Lighten up on the Code, and put the long, gory details in the policy where they belong. More than 25 pages and you're pushing it. It needs to be enticing to read. The point of a Code is to act as a reference guide, a training and awareness tool to set the tone of the company. It needs to be easily read and understood by every level of employee of the company. It's no good if it isn't understood. Make sure the style, tone and language used in the Code is easy to read and reflective of the target audiences. *For the love of all that is good and pure in the world, do not let the lawyers or auditors write the Code!* It needs to be in plain language, not legal, audit or financial-ese!

4. **Closing loop holes.** Rational, logic and thoughtful mind sets are what you are seeking to develop in the company. You cannot possibly write a Code that is 25 pages or less that covers every possible do

and don't in conducting business on a day to day basis. You want your readers THINKING about what they're doing and the decisions they're making and not relying on specifics. See the forest, not only the trees. Trees are in the policy. Otherwise they're just constantly looking for loop holes – so cute... they try to be little lawyers. And some people will live in those loop holes if you let them. I like to get in a few logic and good sense questions which will help close those loop holes. Including something like the questions below.

"Ethical Decision-Making

Ethical decision-making is essential to the success of our Company. Some decisions are obvious and easy to make; *others are not.* When faced with a difficult situation, asking ourselves the questions below can help us to make the right ethical decisions. ***Five "yes" answers are required to qualify an action as ethical and in step with our Company's Core Values.***

1. **Is it legal?**
    If you even *think* an action may be illegal or put the company in liability, do not proceed. If you are not sure, or if you need information about which laws apply in a given situation, talk with your supervisor, manager or our corporate legal staff. Make sure you understand the implications of any laws, regulations or policies that may apply and keep that information in your records as well. You may be asked in the future about a particular issue, and you'll need that information readily available.

2. **Is it consistent with company policy?**
    If the proposed action does not comply with Company policy, you should not do it.

3. **Is it consistent with the Company's Core Values?**
    Consider whether the action would be consistent with our Company's core Values. Sometimes policies and practices may be implemented which go against the Company's core values. In such instances, the policy or practices needs to be reviewed, and possibly reconsidered. But until they are, stick to the values on principal.

4. **If it was in the news tomorrow, would you be comfortable if friends and family saw it?**

   Ask yourself if you would make the same decision if you knew that it would be reported on the front page of tomorrow's newspaper, on YouTube or CNN. Would you behave the same if your family were standing right in front of you?

5. **Could I stand in front of the entire company or a court of law and take responsibility for this action or decision?**

   If you have to hide your decisions, instructions to your subordinates, or actions in any way, ask yourself why. If you think that your actions are actually a secret, think again. In a corporation, there are no such things as secrets. Someone will always know, someone will always find out and someone will always tell."

I like these five questions to help close loopholes. These questions are just headache savers. Instead of arguing with some dumbass on specific language regarding sexual harassment, for example, simply ask the douche-bag if his wife was in the room would he have acted the same way? I had one guy in a training session about Sexual Harassment keep throwing out these stupid scenarios, "What if I do this.." and "What if she does this..". He thought he was being funny and clever. I finally just got fed up and said, 'ask your wife' and pointed behind him. The flash of panic on his face for that split second before logic reminded him that his wife wasn't actually in the room and standing behind him, made my whole week better. He was so professional for the entire remaining workshop time. I desperately wanted to call his wife after that workshop and just give her my condolences. You know, it can't have been easy for her all those years married to such a dickhead; poor thing. And yes, the situation I mentioned actually happened. He thought he was smooth. I swear the pirate wanted to just sit him down in front of a mirror and say, "Really? You're so that confident working with that?" Even the thirsty women in the company thought he was creepy as hell, and he made it worse for himself when he talked in meetings. He'd go on and on about nothing. He just had to speak up and no one was telling him he sounds like an idiot. Five minutes of his voice in a meeting and your brain is screaming, "Make it stop! Kill it! Kill it before it lays eggs!"

5. There needs to be a very clearly written section on **reporting** and the company's **no-retaliation policy.** If you are serious about your compliance program and committed to making it effective, you need to make it as easy as possible to report and make it clear that people are safe to do so. Anyone taking the time to report a concern isn't doing so easily. There is always a fear that it will be traced back to them, that they'll get in trouble for speaking up. That fear is real and based in an ugly reality. It is a risky thing to do. And if they are at the point of facing that risk and making the report, the situation has already gotten bad enough to push them over that line. Your Code needs to make it perfectly clear how easy and safe it is to report, and an iron-clad promise that the company does not allow anyone to suffer retaliation. I know of one instance where a plant operator in a refinery knew of some very serious safety risks that were truly life and death issues. When asked why he would not speak up, he explained that he was from Syria. He had a wife and two daughters with him. And if he lost his job, which meant that his family would have to go back to a war torn country. So it was "better that I face this [risk] than to make my wife and daughters go back to Syria." That broke my heart and horrified me. He had to choose between his life and that safety of his family. Something like this:

> "It takes courage to raise an issue relating to possible violations. We know it can be a difficult decision. That is why we are committed to ensuring that those who do report do not face retaliation, reprisals or any career disadvantage for complying with or reporting potential violations of the Code. Retaliation means any action or behavior done against someone who may or may not have reported a concern with the intention to punish or discourage the safe reporting of violations. This includes, but is not limited to termination of employment, demoting, suspending, threatening, harassing or in any other manner discriminating against anyone who complies with or reports a violation of our policy and is considered retaliation. This is strictly prohibited. The

company will take action against any individuals, at any level, engaging in retaliatory behavior up to and including termination; reporting all incidents of retaliation against a reporter directly to the Board of Directors. Any individual who suspects that they or someone they know has been retaliated against should contact the Compliance Organization immediately."

You can't just promise it is safe and easy, *you have to make it safe and easy*! You do this in the Compliance Policy. You must define, describe and lay out what exactly your company will consider to be retaliation so that there will be no mistaking it or misunderstanding it. Then you need to make it loud and clear with obvious teeth - especially supervisors, managers, executives and officers, that any substantiated claims of retaliation will be reported directly to the board. It is the one issue that no matter the level of the offender, the board will hear about it. A corporate culture that allows for retaliation will kill your compliance program's reporting mechanism and destroy any trust you had or hope to build in management. It is the fastest way to turn employees into assassins and pirates overnight. People are not going to take a bullet for a company that won't protect them. Why should they? Be warned, Swans, Mini-Kings, and Egos will retaliate against reporters – it is their nature to protect themselves and not the company. It will be all they have left if they failed to stop the compliance program to begin with. Also consider this; there are law firms out there who make money representing whistleblowers in reporting corruption. The SEC Whistleblower Act also offers whistleblower rewards to those individuals who report original information about violations of the Foreign Corrupt Practices Act (FCPA). A potential Foreign Corrupt Practices Act whistleblower can receive as a financial reward between 10% and 30% of any penalty imposed by the SEC.

Consider the following as well: under the 2010 Dodd-Frank Act the whistleblower can remain anonymous.

Whistleblowers are eligible for rewards if the *recovery* is over a million dollars but the US law enforcement agencies like Department of Justice ("DOJ") and the Security Exchange Commission ("SEC") can make a payout on the amount *collected*, even if it is less than a million dollars.

The DOJ and SEC whistleblower program is a success. *"We're seeing high-quality tips that are saving our investigators substantial time and resources,"* said SEC Chairman Mary L. Schapiro. If a whistleblower from your company doesn't feel reporting to your hotline is safe or will benefit anyone, they will eventually go outside and report. The possibility of getting several hundred thousands of dollars or more as a reward – they won't give a shit if you fire them or retaliate then. They might think about it for a second, while giggling and sipping a fruity drink out of a coconut shell with a little umbrella sticking out on a beach in the Maldives – enjoying the payout - but not much after that.

Keep your hotline anonymous, effective, safe and easy. Because sooner or later, that dirty laundry is going to be aired, and you will regret it immensely when it gets aired in court or the media when is could have been dealt with internally if your hotline was better.

Many companies list their **values or mission language** at the beginning of the Code and then are done with that. DON'T miss the opportunity to reinforce those values *throughout the entire code*. Take every opportunity to reuse those same value catch words throughout the Code in bold lettering. This will drive the point home further when they see those words over and over and over and over again. Words like **Integrity, Accountability, Trust, Diversity, Transparency, Employees, Customers, Ownership, Fairness, etc.** Then for the rest of the entire texts in the Code make sure those words are bolded to not-so-subtly remind the reader that this is an important value to the company and you want it to mean as much to the reader.

6. The **subjects or topic** covered in nearly all Codes of Conduct is pretty much the same. But it really shouldn't be. *Keep the subjects limited to the specific risks your company, in your industry and in your part of the world is facing.* If your company is not a listed company, you may want to limit the section on Insider Trading or leave that out of the Topic Headings altogether but remember to put in a section under confidentiality about having access to information of other companies that may be clients, business associates, vendors, etc. and that all non-public information is considered confidential – not to be utilized or shared and *then* relate it to insider trading. Mold your Codes to your company, and brand it. Make it yours.

7. When writing the Code, don't just go section by section with dos and don'ts. Use **comprehension aides** like charts, Q&A's, FAQ bubbles, examples and case studies. Separate these aids from the regular text. Make sure they stand out to get the special attention they need. These aids can really bring the message home for your readers.

8. The finished product should be look like something even a picky employee will be happy to have on their desk. It should have a **polished, sexy, final presentation and style,** fonts, stylish layout, etc. In selecting pictures, test-drive them with a few employees with fresh eyes. See if the pictures are relatable to the subject of that section, provoke a positive emotional response, are relevant to the time and corporate culture. I hate seeing a section of a Code about equal opportunity employment with a picture of a sunrise over a mountain. Yeah, pretty picture! Who doesn't like a good mountain sunrise, but what the fuck has that got to do with a promise not to discriminate? Keep the written language and visual aids on the same subject at all times. You want to use as many different senses and sections of the brain (emotional, logic, language, visual, etc.) simultaneously soaking in all of the Code's messages to ensure it as deeply engrained in their memory as possible. It should make resistance to the Code's messages futile. Resistance is futile.

If you have a good public relations and graphics team, use them! Keep a close reign on them so they don't fuck up the subliminal Borg mind control messages you've carefully, secretly embedded into the text, but let them use their expertise and make it *sexy*. By sexy, I mean something appealing that people want to pick up, look at, read, finger through and over again and again. A trusted book of reference and resource; it is your company's gospel.

Take a note here. The best graphics team can make a mediocre code look like a diamond. But if the content of the code is shitty, it won't matter how good they are. You can't polish a turd.

9. The last page of your Code should be *a copy* of the **Acknowledgement or Integrity Pledge**, or whatever you want to call it. When the employee is given their new hire orientation and on-boarding process, the Code will have been given to them *and they will have had training on it*. That

Acknowledgement or Integrity Pledge is a separate page they will be asked to sign and hand over to show that they have received, read and understood the Code thereby removing any excuses to not report or not know how to behave and conduct themselves in the company. That first Acknowledgement is their first year's certification in Ethics & Compliance. They will get a new one each year when they do the 20 minute e-learning Compliance course to recertify.

These points need to be mostly focused on in your Corporate Code of Conduct. The other Code of Conduct is the **Supplier's Code of Conduct.** The Supplier's Code of Conduct is a different creature. It looks and sounds a lot like the Corporate Code but it is shorter, has fewer pictures, but still has the Acknowledgement at the end. This not signed by employees. Supplier's codes are signed by any company, contractor, vendor, supplier, etc. that wishes to do business with your company. If they want to contract business with your company they must first be informed of your company's compliance values and policy, they agree to abide by them and then they must show that they've received a copy of the Supplier's Code, they read, understood and agree to abide by them and they fully accept and understand that if they fuck up, they may lose the privilege of making money in business with you. Does this mean they will sign it and you have single handedly ended corruption? No. It does mean that when you suppliers or vendors do fuck up, you can put your hands up and say, "We're not with them." You are doing only what you can to make it clear that you value compliance with law and regulation and if they screw up, you can say you had no knowledge of it, nor do you condone it, etc.

While codes of conduct all pretty much have the same content, they do need to be tailored for your company within the guide lines above. But there is no need to reinvent the wheel. Go take a look at the codes for companies that are in the same industry as your company and see what they've got. Don't copy verbatim. Have a little self-respect and pride and shoot for better. Better language, better graphics, better readability, and I am a huge advocate for including references to specific laws of the country and industry you're in. If you're an international company with agents and representatives in other countries you'll need to be careful to make sure of jurisdiction.

I've put in some points on a standard Code of Conduct below. But this is not a finished product. It is a starting point where you take out the areas that are not relevant to your company's particular liability, elaborate on areas where your company is at a higher risk, and make it ... sexy. Yes, it has to be so sexy that your employees want to look at it. They will feel compelled to pick it up, thumb through its pages and read it, over and over and over again.

It might be nice if I just gave you a sample to copy, but in all truth, it is best to just give each company things to consider. It is also a good idea to take a good look at the codes of the best companies in your particular industry. Google 'corruption' and add your industry. Then do the same exercise for your region. See the risks inherent to your industry and region. Then work those risks into the areas you need to develop the most for your own code. Here are some other considerations:

❖ **Company's Core Values**

Insert the company's core values, mission, vision, or whatever else floats your boat. Warning! If your management is not perceived by employees to actually represent or embrace the company's values themselves, don't include them. Nothing pisses off employees more than a bunch of hypocritical assholes talking about values their behavior proves they know nothing about. If you want to increase the likelihood of employees retaliating against the company, losing any last grain of respect they may have had for management and refusing to give the values a chance of actually becoming part of the corporate culture, then management should truly represent those values or shut the fuck up about them.

❖ **About *[Company Name]*'s Code of Conduct**

Using the Code – talk about what you expect people get from the code. What message is it supposed to send? What laws and regulations do you want to be constantly at the foremost of your employees' minds while they conduct business and act on your company's behalf?

❖ *Ethical Decision-Making*

Explain a little about the difference between ethics and compliance and what measuring stick or standard do you want your employees to use when making the determination that even if something is legal to do, is it ethical? I recommend using the 'YES' questions at the beginning of this section.

❖ Anonymous Reporting a Possible Violation of our Code of Conduct

Clearly define who is responsible for administering the compliance program. Is it a compliance organization? The General Auditor? The General Counsel? Who they are, and all of the ways employees and outside parties can either report a concern or get questions answered, anonymously. Make it easy to get the phone number, hotlines, emails, snail mail, internet hotlines (recommended), etc. for your compliance organization.

❖ No Retaliation Policy

Write out both your definition of retaliation – what it is and what it does. Then spell out the details of your policy on retaliation explaining what are protected and legal actions (reporting legit concerns, asking questions, even complaining about the boss). And explain what are not protected, like filing false claims or reports, defamation or slander, etc. Note to management: if it's true, it ain't slander or defamation baby! It's you getting exposed! This is the worst place in your code or program to say it and not mean it. This is a critical aspect of your compliance policy to make sure that when you say people are safe from retaliation, that every person in the company especially management understands that you fucking mean it. You won't tolerate it. You won't allow it. You will punish for it. This is vitally crucial to your program's strength. This is its oxygen. If you're not prepared to protect this, then just forget it. The tone from the top (Shareholder, Board, executives, management, to employees) and back up again from the employees. Employees can retaliate against the company's management for shit as well.

❖ Company's Reputation

Explain just how important your company's reputation is to you. Go into how it is for the company's best interest and its employees' best interest to do everything possible to protect the company, because its people ARE THE COMPANY. Bring your employees into the fold! If your management cannot fully wrap their heads around the fact that a company is a living, breathing, ever changing organism, and a sum of its parts – just like a living body. The parts are every single employee. So what hurts the employees hurts the company. What hurts the company; hurts the employees. If you fail to make that connection clear and an essential part of corporate culture – go home.

❖ Compliance

Make the written and public commitment to be compliant with all the laws and regulations. Set a standard for all employees to conduct their business within the laws, regulations and policies of the company. Compliance simply means the company and its employees follow the laws and regulations it is required to. Company policies and practices and standards of operations MUST BE WRITTEN, TRAINED ON, ENFORCED AND REINFORCED with full compliance of the laws. If the policies say one thing, and there is a law that says something else, then you're not in compliance.

Here is a good example for Saudi Arabian companies.

- Article 3 of the Saudi labor law says employment is the equal right to all citizens. This means male AND female citizens. There is no differentiation between an employee's obligations to employers based on gender. (I know someone is already thinking about maternity leave and hazardous work. And I know that you're a Saudi.)
- Article 26 of the Saudi Labor Law requires companies to employee a minimum of 75% of its manpower as Saudi nationals.
- Article 149 says, "Women may not unless protected by specific restrictions be employed in dangerous, risky or potentially harmful work, as defined in resolutions to be issued by the Ministry of Labor." For a list of restricted jobs, see: Ministerial Report No. 1/738 dated

04 July 2004 – Restricted Jobs for Women. The list includes working with fusion ovens, explosives, operating a jack hammer, and other shitty hard labor jobs no women in Saudi wants anyways. So, being an operator in a refinery is out of the questions. But working in an office in a refining company is just fine. Hey, its Saudi.

- Saudi Royal Decree No. 25, Article 11, dated 28/08/1421 h (05/28/2000 g) concerning the ratification of the United Nations Convention to Ending Discrimination Against Women, clearly states that you cannot discriminate against women in jobs, benefits, allowances, etc.

I put all of these specific references here to make a point. What is the point? Well, there a lot of companies in Saudi say they are equal opportunity employers but are they really? Many don't even hire women. Including some US companies. BIG US companies! US Companies are supposed to follow US laws in employment and business. But then again, the labor issues are different when they incorporate overseas. They have subsidiaries in Saudi. You can identify them. The company name will show up as 'US Company Arabia' or 'US Company Middle East'. They do this because while the US companies have a strict set of laws and regulations they have to abide by, like not discriminating against women; the subsidiary doesn't. So if Article 3 says employment is an equal right to all citizens, but some companies don't even hire women or specify non-hazardous jobs for 'males only', are they compliant with the law? Nope. Is the Saudi Ministry of Labor enforcing this law? Nope. So companies don't feel any need to abide by it. If you're not going to abide by it, don't claim that you are in your code. That makes you a liar, and a dumbass because people will know you don't abide by it and you're NOT actually and equal opportunity employer.

The 75% requirement? That is called Saudization. It's a form of an affirmative action. And do companies abide by it? They do comply, or they work very hard to make it look like they do. They will either actually have 75% of their employees as Saudi nationals, or in the case of smaller companies, they will hire Saudis on paper, give them a minimum salary to stay at home, and then go hire as many expatriate workers as they want. Usually other Arab nationals from war torn countries, or Filipinos or Indians or Pakistanis. People they can abuse and pay shit wages to. The minimal payment to those fake Saudi employees is only about 2,000 Saudi riyals (about US$250.00). Why comply with this 75% rule and not so much Article 3? Because the government is enforcing this one.

Article 149 is just an article used to explain why women cannot work in one job or another and most companies I've come across have never seen the actual list in Ministerial Report No. 1/738. They don't want to. What about Royal Decree No. 25? Do companies comply with that? Nope. Women are routinely denied benefits based on gender. There are actually women in Saudi who qualify as heads of household with dependents as defined in another Saudi Law the Saudi Cooperative Health Insurance Law. The law defines what a dependent is and makes it clear that a woman can be the head of the house hold. But how many companies will give a woman the contract type or benefits of an employee with dependants? I've only seen one in 20 years in Saudi and that was given as an out of policy exception.

On another note, there is also a Saudi Royal Decree against racial discrimination. Saudi Royal Decree No. M/12 of 16/4/1418 h. ratifying International Convention on the Elimination of all Forms of Racial Discrimination. It is a Saudi law. BUT a practice throughout the entire country to pay Western expatriate workers, up to three or four times as much as Saudi nationals. While Asians and other Arab (the other Arab nationals from Egypt, Syria, Lebanon, etc, or Filipinos or Indians or Pakistanis, etc.) their salaries can be as low as $1/10^{th}$ of a Saudis. So an American Engineer with 3 years of experience can be paid about US$ 10,000 a month. A Saudi Engineer with 30 years' experience will be paid about the same, but with only three years' experience will be paid about a third of that.

A Filipino or Indian or Pakistani will make only about a third, and they could have a higher degree of a masters or PhD, and decades of experience. They will always be paid disgustingly lower in the Middle East because of their race. There is a law against racial discrimination, but it isn't enforced. And they don't give a shit to enforce it because they are getting experience labor, cheap as fuck and it's a racist culture. They don't build their own houses. They don't pick up their own trash. And they don't make their own tea. The brown people from other Arab or Asian countries shit salaries to do it for them. The point is, don't put in your code that you're going to be fair, compliant or equal unless you are.

❖ Controlled Substance and Drugs

This seems like it should be a no brainer, but it isn't. Of course you need to spell out your no tolerance policy for illegal and controlled substances. *You also need to add in a section about legal and prescription drugs.* If an employee is taking a prescription or even an over the counter drug that warns NOT to operate heavy equipment while taking the drug, do you really want this employee to show up to work?

What about employees who are taking or could possibly take prescribed drugs for chronic conditions like diabetes, epilepsy, or other illnesses? Normally, employers in industrial companies in which safety concerns on the job or in plants will need to be extra careful in monitoring prescription medications. Are you going to require a disclosure from employees? What are the consequences for not disclosing?

❖ Responsibilities of Leaders

Being a supervisor or in a management role means more money, more responsibility and a higher level of accountability. It is not, and should never be a 'get out of jail' card which means you can break the rules you'd punish employees for and not hold yourselves accountable. This is a one way ticket to a vote of no confidence in management if management is not held to the same or higher standard of behavior.

❖ Personal Data

Employees will have access to personal data like addresses, salaries, benefits, family information, etc. What is going to be your standard of expectation and consequences if an employee with access to that information accesses it for non-business purposes?

❖ Workplace Violence and Harassment

Define what you will consider violence and harassment, and be sure to do your homework here! What are the discrimination and harassment laws where you are? What are the company's obligations under those laws? Your jurisdictional regulations have to be embedded into your Codes and your Policies.

❖ Company Records and Internal Controls

Accurate books and records are essential for managing your business. More companies have been fined for corruption based on skewed numbers, forged or falsified reports, or just careless half-ass reporting. Have a standard, a clear and well laid out policy and process for EVERYTHING. If you can assign a money amount to any report, then make sure it is prepared by one organization, checked by another, and verified and SIGNED by the proper company authorities. If your accounting and reporting methods are so loose that no one is willing to sign their name to them, confirming their lack of confidence in them, then you have issues.

❖ Corruption

This is a broad heading. You will need to break it down into subsections and give as brief but inclusive explanation of what your company defines as corruption for specific subheading here. Define it, reference the law or regulation or government guideline, state your level of tolerance for and then lay down the consequences for it in your company. Consequences include disciplinary actions, suspension, company fines, termination, reporting the matter to the authorities, and legal action directly from the company against individual(s) who engage in corrupt business practices. Say it. State it. Mean it. Train it. ENFORCE IT. Having your company's clearly stated position on corruption laid out, and enforced means that not only are you teaching the rules, the confidence of employees in the company's intention to enforce the rules regarding corruption can be a major deterrent. Once your management bends the rules here and there, the deviance from your compliance policy becomes the standard behavior. Once you've started down that path, your legal team will spend more time putting out fires then working on operational development or performance improvement. The more deviant behavior in your company, the higher your damn legal bills will be. If your management can't figure out that obvious correlation between bad behavior and millions being spent in legal fees, then they're either fucking idiots or the ones engaging in the bad behavior.

❖ Conflicts of Interest

A lot of people mistakenly think conflict of interests is not that big of a deal and fail to really take steps to educate about it, or prevent it. So many companies in the Middle East require an annual, routine conflict of interest form for employees to fill out and that is the extent of their preventative measures. It is a lazy ass, uninformed, and stupid process which does not protect anyone – especially the company. The subject of Conflicts of interest needs to be trained on. There are different areas which aren't going to be perfectly clear to everyone. There are a lot of grey areas when it comes to conflict of interests. The rule of thumb is that if you're making a business decision based on something that serves your interests and not on the company's, that is a conflict of interest.

That personal interest could be for your own financial gain, personal or career gain, or to prevent a financial loss, or to prevent the personal or career loss to yourself, a family or friend, etc.

If you are in a company where there are long-time friend or family associations in the company, same industry or same area, then you need to be very cautious. Disclosures should be made on an annual basis as a backup but with the understanding that all disclosures need to be made in writing, and as they come up – not only on the annual disclosure form. Even giving someone a job or a promotion or special treatment at the company because of who their father is a lot like JP Morgan's Sons & Daughters Program in China. It is a little like nepotism, except that people are hiring others' kin; not their own. In the Middle East, it's called the *Who's Yo Daddy* Program; in Arabic ‘*wasta*’.

It is all about meeting someone powerful or influential, giving their kid or spouse or other family member a job they are probably not qualified for, then holding that favor as a ‘marker’ for any future request for help or favor you may have in the future. If Daddy is an executive it won't be long before the kids and younger siblings start showing up on the man power list – and are fast tracked to management training courses and development opportunities that others work damn hard for but never get. If anyone ever asks how a particularly inept individual managed to get such a good position, good salary or power, others will answer in a single word, wasta. Then it is understood.

There is good wasta and bad. Good wasta will get you an interview and the chance to prove you're qualified for the job. Bad wasta will get you the job even when you're not. It will keep the individual from any disciplinary action, even when they deserve it. It will allow them to behave in any way they want without ever having to be held accountable. It puts their immediate management at a huge disadvantage because a bullet proof wasta'd employee makes the whole organization tense. They don't have to perform, while others pick up the slack. They get special favors, protections and developmental opportunities others will never be given. If they are enough of a nightmare to deal with, they'll be promoted just to get them out of the department. They will be resented by their colleagues, and never really earn the respect of well, anyone. If other workers feel that it doesn't matter how hard they work, they'll never have the wasta needed to succeed, they disengage and stop producing. They'll only work hard to leave.

❖ Gift and favors and bribes

You really cannot skip this part; any of this part. JP Morgan got into a lot of very deep and ultimately expensive trouble with their Sons & Daughters program in China. They hired family members of Chinese leaders at 75% of their Chinese firms it took public from 2004 to 2013. This is bribery, in the form of a 'favor', Giving hiring preferences in the Middle East is called 'wasta'; and it is bribery. Gifts can be trips, tickets, other material gifts not normally given as marketing tools like pens, cups and calendars with the company logo. Some company's give better gifts, but a simple rule of thumb is that if it isn't mass produced and have the giver's logo on it, don't take it. Gifts are meant to seem innocuous, but their sole purpose is to influence preferential decision making.

A faux 'consulting contract' for your relative, is a bribe. On the 29th of November 2013, Arab News published an article on line that Alstom was awarded nine contracts with Saudi Electric Company.[1] On December 22, 2014 the US Department of Justice News announced that Alstom plead guilty

---

[1]   Arab News. (2013)" **Alstom Grid contracts support Saudi energy boom.** Available at: **h**ttp://www.arabnews.com/news/484551

to violations of the Foreign Corrupt Practices Act and paid a $772 million in criminal charges.

> *"According to the companies' admissions, Alstom, Alstom Prom, Alstom Power and Alstom Grid, through various executives and employees, paid bribes to government officials and falsified books and records in connection with power, grid and transportation projects for state-owned entities around the world, including in Indonesia, Egypt, Saudi Arabia, the Bahamas and Taiwan."* [2]

That is a favourite way of helping friends and family; getting them contracts with the company you work in. Contracts for services never rendered, consulting never given, materials that are worth a shit, and knock offs that are so bad, they'll cost you more to move them out to the trash that what they'll actually be worth.

Sometimes, the company will pay a bribe in a % of each body they provide for companies or projects. You will find this a lot in manpower contracts for supplementary manpower, contractors, inspectors, etc. Individuals will push hard for specific companies to be selected; the contracting processes are not stringent enough to keep the bidding process clean or managed well. Justifications for selecting one company over another are either non-existent or bullshit.

Contracting processes in the Middle East leave much, very much to be desired. Supply chain management with good compliance due diligence is nearly non-existent. Here is a good place for me to sing the praises of Thomas Reuter's World Check. For a small subscription fee, a company can add this due diligence step into their bidding process to come up with a ranking system for companies bidding for contracts. It literally takes SECONDS to do a fast risk management check for any company or consultant. If I was an anti-corruption law enforcement agency in the Middle East, I'd find ways to audit

---

[2] US Department of Justice News (2014). **"Alstom Pleads Guilty and Agrees to Pay $772 Million Criminal Penalty to Resolve Foreign Bribery Charges"** Available at: https://www.justice.gov/opa/pr/alstom-pleads-guilty-and-agrees-pay-772-million-criminal-penalty-resolve-foreign-bribery

the contracting processes and double check on change orders for a contract to find all sorts of little goodies – or bad behavior. Just saying.... That is where I'd look.

❖ Insider Trading

This should absolutely be included in the code for publicly traded companies as well as companies who have contracts with publicly traded companies or a shareholder who is a publicly traded company. Cite the appropriate laws and regulations which have jurisdiction, define what insider trading is, give examples and lay out the consequences very clearly for those who break the rules. Those consequences MUST include turning over violations to the authorities. Without all of these, it's a half-ass code and policy.

❖ Safety, Health, Environment and Security

A lot of codes have no more than a blurb about these subtopics. You need more; especially if your company is in a high risk industry. Explain your company's commitment to these points; state the specific rules, regulations, laws and STANDARDS. Define what you consider a violation, and the consequences for violating them. This must include violations on reporting documents. For safety violations in the company, the company must commit to declaring and rectifying any and all safety violations; at least internally. You need to make safety concerns and practices a normal part of your daily discussions. And always remember that talk is fucking cheap. If you talk about safety and then don't punish those who violate safety standards, no one will take you seriously when you're talking about it. They will politely listen when the management talks about safety, and then do nothing because they will know you're full of shit and it's just talk.

When discussing health, you have to think of risks to employees' health while at work and outside of work. Does your health insurance coverage include annual check-ups and preventative care? Do you have programs for smoking, high blood pressure, breast cancer or other types of cancer? What kinds of health related awareness programs are you running?

The environment is all covered by laws and regulations of whatever country you're operating in. I cannot tell you how hypocritical it is to see and hear a company talk about best practices or throw phrases around like 'best in class' and then violate the environmental standards and regulations for their country. Best practices are based off of recognized standards set by recognized standard setting organizations – like governments. Best practices are never set by other companies or consultants! The term best in class is stupid. What class? Best company in your industry? Really? Can you prove it? Best in class for your country? Really? How do you compare your company in your industry to a different company in a different industry? Best in class in your region? Can you show that? Personally, I am suspicious of any company who says they are the best in class and fails to mention the specific class. If there are 10 ugly, stupid and lewd people sitting at a table, and you are the least ugly, least stupid and least lewd, then you are the best in class for that class. Can you set a little higher and more stringent goal?

If you have to deal with air emissions, water contaminations, land, etc. Find out what the minimum requirements or standards are and at least meet them. If that is all the commitment and effort you're willing to put forth, then at least that is something. No complaints. BUT if you want to talk about best practices, then meet the minimums and strive for the highest standards available. Don't lie or skew the numbers on your own testing. Remember, if at least one person knows you're dumping or littering or poisoning the ground water with leaking chemicals or polluting the air, the truth will eventually come out. Walk the talk. Don't bullshit. State your company's commitment, cite the laws and live up to it.

❖ Anti-Trust and Fair Competition

If your company has competitors, has contracts for good and services with companies who are competitors with each other, or basically conducts business anywhere in the world in any industry, you must include Anti-Trust and Fair Competition in your code. This will set the standard for how your company operates fairly from every aspect to what it buys, sells, and who it hires. Make sure you cite the relevant laws and regulations and give examples of what would be a violation of it. Even something as simple as a gentlemen's agreement with another company not to hire their employees is a violation of law. It artificially caps the employment market / salaries for people in your country or in a particular field. It is a despicable practice that hurts more people than most actually realize. Anything that keeps salaries and job opportunities capped is bad for the market.

Other subtitles in a code could include:

- Intellectual Property
- Protection of confidential information
- Access and use of the company's internet and software
- Records Management
- Proper use and access to the company's resources
- Government Affairs
- Public Relations
- Social Media
- Labor Relations and Human Rights (yes, they are directly related!)

❖ Administration of the Code

Like I explained earlier, the who or what organization in your company is responsible for the administration of your compliance program and code of conduct? You need to clarify this by naming the organization; who is the head of that organization, and who do they report to. For a really transparent organization, you'd even add in the contact information for the Board of Directors. That is a way to make it abundantly clear that your company takes its commitment to compliance so seriously that if the organization responsible for administering the program and the code fucks up, you can go straight to the board and let them know. That is confidence right there!

❖ Acknowledgement

As explained earlier, the final section in your code is the part that the employee acknowledges that they've received the code, read it, been trained on it and are pledging to abide by it. This should be done for new employee orientations, and all employees should be recertified on compliance annually after that. Eliminate the possibility of "I didn't' know" excuse for misbehavior.

SUPPLIERS CODE OF CONDUCT

The Supplier's Code is usually a much shorter code, and it is given to EVERY company, consultant, or third party that you have a contract with; any kind of contract. A supplier's codes should include the following:

- ❖ Message from [the company]
- ❖ Compliance with Laws, Codes and Regulations
- ❖ Environmental, Health, and Safety Practices
- ❖ Ethical Business Practice
  - o Fair Trade Practice
  - o Ethical Sourcing
  - o Relationships and Communications
  - o Bribery, Kickbacks and Fraud
  - o Gifts, Gratuities and Hospitality
- ❖ Monitoring and Compliance
- ❖ Office of Ethics & Compliance
- ❖ Confidentiality
- ❖ Application
- ❖ Acknowledgment of the company's Supplier Code of Conduct.

All codes should be available in English, the native language of the country it is registered or operates in – if not in English. The supplier's code should also be available in every language of every country the company does business in. This is a basic thing and not an extra step. Your codes are no good unless they're understood. If a company wants to do business with your company, they should be required to sign the supplier's code or forget about doing business with you.

Here are the tricky parts of the Supplier's Code if you didn't already have one and are trying to implement a compliance program – (1) your existing contracted suppliers are obviously not obligated to sign, and (2) some suppliers are not going to want to sign any 'additional' requirements outside of the contract. Existing suppliers already have a contractual agreement with you and are under no obligation to change that contract for the duration of the contract term.

Here is what I suggest. Send a copy of the supplier's code with a formal letter to all of your existing suppliers, vendors and third parties (anyone you have a contract with) explaining how the company is in the process of implementing a compliance program and that from now on any new suppliers will be required sign the acknowledgement of the supplier's code before being considered as an approved supplier to the company. However since they [*the supplier you're writing to*] are already a "valued business partner" your company wishes to inform them of its efforts in meeting its compliance requirements. Ask them if they have any issues in agreeing to the contents of the supplier's code and in the most polite, diplomatic manner possible let them know that only suppliers who can meet those expectations will be considered favorably upon renewal of any existing contracts. In a very nice way you're trying to let them know that if they cannot agree to abide by the supplier's code, the relationship may be over after the existing contract ends. You will not renew their contract. Stick to your guns on this! AND, again, if a vendor / supplier refuse to sign, or there is no record of them signing and yet somehow still managed to get renewed…. Start looking into who is renewing and any inappropriate relationship that might possibly exist.

This is how you are protecting your company from liability and deniability from shady third parties. You cannot control what third parties do in their company. You cannot control how they run their business. If they engage in shady business practices and get busted for it – *and everyone gets busted sooner or later* – your liability can be reduced because you can show your company's efforts towards implementing a compliance program and your effort to make that commitment clear to your third parties in the supplier's code acknowledgement. Don't go about this half-ass either. Commit to it like hot waxing the sensitive areas! Once you've started the process, you're in it!

If your company's name appears in the media as having accepted bribes to award contracts or associated with shady dealing at all, your company is in a better position to do reputational and legal damage control. The signed acknowledgement is a piece of paper but it is a piece of paper which says 'these are our rules' and they agreed to it. Companies with compliance programs, *with good compliance programs – not bullshit for show only compliance programs*, who have gotten busted for violating corruption laws, almost always get greatly reduced fines and sometimes the company gets off the hook completely and only individuals get snagged. That is what you want! If individuals break the rules – rules of either the corporate code or supplier's code, the individuals need to take the heat and be held accountable for their own actions.

- Rule #1. Protect the company! Protect the shareholders!
- Rule #2. Protect the company! Protect the shareholders!
- Rule #3. Protect the company! Protect the shareholders!
- Rule #4. Let dumb fucktards who break the rules hang out to dry for their own stupid ass decisions and illicit behavior! Let bad eggs fry, and don't do it quietly! Make sure everyone in the company can see there is no tolerance for illicit behavior.
- Rule #5. Protect the company! Protect the shareholders!

What hurts the company and the shareholders hurts everyone. The reputation of the company needs to be strong. Money spent on criminal and civil fines paying for those dumbass's mistakes, could be spent on training, development, salary increases, office improvements, bonuses; basically anything that benefits all of your employees' wellbeing and work environment. It should not be wasted on covering the ass of people who didn't give a fuck about the company in the first place. If they gave a fuck, they wouldn't have engaged in risky behavior that is likely to cost the shareholders and the company (employees) in the end. I am always suspicious of a board or executives who protect and cover non-compliance of others. Makes them look like maybe, just maybe, they got something to hide as well. So they are afraid of holding others responsible because maybe they will be exposed as well. Wanna look guilty? Stand by the guilty.

Once your compliance program is in place, then you can require any new suppliers, vendors, service providers, and third parties you will be contracting with to sign the supplier code acknowledgement. If the language of the supplier's code turns out to be prohibitive or an obstacle to negotiations, you can shorten it to the Acknowledgement section and then work the rest of the language into the company's boiler plate language of your contracts and agreements under an anti-corruption section. You will still encounter suppliers who are hesitant to sign and get on board with the compliance program, but those are the suppliers you can do without. And remember what we said in the first part? Who doesn't want a compliance program or compliance measures in the company and contracting processes? The kind of people and organizations you don't want to do business with anyway! Fuck 'em!

5

Compliance Policy

Compliance Policies really aren't hard to do. Take the Code of Conduct, and then in each section you highlight the text that is in the Code in one color making it stand out. Then in normal black text, you add to it any specific laws and procedures related to that particular subject of the Code. Or you can add in foot note references to specific laws and regulations that guide your Compliance Program's restrictions – you'll be referencing laws that you are compelled to follow due to jurisdiction, etc.

In the Section on Reporting, you'll explain to whom and how to report concerns in the Code, but in the additional text you'll name the proponent or compliance organization, and under whose authority and by what vehicle they administer the compliance program. Is this a board approval under a Unanimous Written Consent that the compliance organization exists and has the power to act on the policy and report to the board. You will need a section which outlines the duties of the head of the compliance organization, the other staff in the organization, and the other company organizations who will appoint a representative to the Corporate Compliance Committee. What the Committee members' requirements are and how they are allowed to operate under this committee. You will need to define your company's self-reporting policy.

Not to be confused with a reporting hotline, you need to define what kinds of items will be reported to the authorities under different laws. If a crime occurs in the company, and it becomes known by the management, what and who are they required to officially report to inform of the issues, define what the company is going to do to resolve the issues.

This is important to note! Case history of other companies that have self-reported is that the law enforcement agencies were more understanding and lenient. It's the companies that try to hide or fight jurisdiction that get it the worst – not those who've self-reported. It will hurt worse if you struggle.

I've gotten more than a few surprised expressions from some companies – in the Middle East and even in the US, when I mentioned a self-declaration policy. "Do we have to?" Yes *Poindexter*! You do have to report crimes to the authorities. That is kind of the rule EVERY WHERE IN THE WORLD. If you found a dead body in your living room do you have to call the police? Yes, of course your do. A crime has occurred on your premises. Otherwise it looks like you're guilty of murder. You wouldn't just bury it in the back yard! A crime is a crime, is a crime, is a crime! And I know there are a lot of corporate lawyers that are going to disagree here and say there are times to self-report and times not to self-report. I am not going to give legal advice, I am only going to say, 'a crime is a crime, is a crime, is a crime'. Any corporate lawyer who disagrees with me is the same kind of lawyer that makes law enforcement view corporate lawyers like mafia lawyers. And nothing stays hidden in a corporation for long, so the company's executives need to decide how deep of a hole is needed to bury the evidence or themselves. Truth will out! Somebody knows, and somebody will rat your asses out. Even the mafia has to worry about rats and snitches. So unless you're going to start tying up loose ends by 'offing' a few employees here and there to make a point, be prepared because someone is going to eventually talk.

The compliance policy will need to lay out the process and steps of how the company receives hotline reports, what is considered a trigger event, how to benchmark your reporting hotline, etc. and what will cause an internal investigation to ensue and what will not, how and when a recommendation is made to the management for decisions, how and who will make the decisions, and how the documentation will be managed and administered. Don't leave out details, because no matter how good the intentions are, if you leave something open to interpretation someone is going to come along later and fuck up the machinery with their own cockeyed interpretations of what they think should be done. Idiot fuck-ups who think they can reinvent the wheel.

The procedure of internal investigations – who will lead, who will make reports, who will be case manager, who will conduct interviews, who will finish the report; each step will need to be laid out in the Compliance policy along with any forms for the investigation that will be needed. The possible consequences for Code violations and the level of hierarchy involved for decisions in charges against managers or executives will all need to be laid out. There should be no guessing involved when an investigation is conducted. Investigations must always, always be conducted 'by the book' so obviously there needs to be *an actual fucking book*!

6

Policy Management

Policy management is the process in which a company's policies are drafted, developed, approved, disseminated, trained on, reviewed annually and enforced throughout the company. Training and enforcing the policies (rules and regulations) of the organization is a major component of a compliance program. However, they are often the most ignored aspect of a company. Not the policies necessarily, but the related Processes and Procedures. You get what you train for, and a burned child fears the flame more.

While I am talking about 'Policies' let me be clear not to confuse them with 'Procedures or Processes'. These words are often interchanged and must be considered distinct types of documents. They may be closely related but each has a unique purpose.

And policy management on a company portal doesn't mean dumping a ton of documents on a company portal site called Policies and Procedures and leaving them there to become ancient and forgotten history. Having a lot of documents in your portal may look like you're doing your job, but it isn't. It's the equivalent of cleaning house by stuffing everything in the damn closet! The house may look clean but it isn't. You'll have a lot of mess in the closet but you won't be able to find anything, and when you do it will be out dated and out of style. Make it a point to clean out your closet on a regular basis. Keep only the policies, processes and procedures that are current and in use now. Keep the old stuff in a department available in *.pdf upon request.

Policies are the business rules and guidelines of a company that may either be based on a specific law or regulation or may be based on purely business decisions for the benefit of the company. Keep in mind, your business decisions cannot contradict what the law says. Policies are the rules and authorities which a company's functions, departments, divisions or sections will be allowed to operate. Policies define **what** the rules are, **who** is responsible for its executions, and the **why**. Policies are the '**governance**', the guidelines under which procedures and processes are written. Policies alone are not enough to guide the organization because they do not completely cover every step of the structured process.

While I am on the subject of policies, let's start by giving an actual definition of the words.

Policies and Procedures Defined

A policy is a set of principles and related guidelines that a company establishes to define its long-term goals, direct and limit the scope of its actions in pursuit of long-term goals, and to protect its interests. Policies are based on laws, regulations, company by-laws, and the company's business interests.

A procedure is a fixed manner of completing a task that consists of a sequence of steps that must be followed in order for the task to be completed properly, and in accordance with the policy.

The reason this needs to be defined, is because if you ask ten people what is a policy and what a procedure is, you'll get ten different fucking answers. I say this because some companies think a policy only has to be a picture on the wall that says something warm and fuzzy like, "It's our policy to protect the environment" or "attract and retain the best talent" or "be good boys and girls!" Those are not actually policies; they are *No Shit Sherlock!' (NSS)* goals. They are really nice objectives to have but since they don't lay out a definite course of action or define a set of principals in detailed guidelines *which can be controlled, measured, standardized, audited*, etc. It does not constitute an actual policy, or the required procedure needed to map out the way to stay in compliance with the 'policy'. Basically, you are going to have to make decisions on a daily basis of how to run your business. The owners of the company want it run in a certain way, and your policies need to reflect specifically how the owners want the business run, who is they authorize to run it and within the confines of law and regulations to keep their asses out of the courtroom and jail. To ensure that it is run safely, productively, consistently and fairly, you need to define how certain decisions are going to be played out.

One of my favorite *NSS policies* to pick apart is the general 'It is our policy to achieve and maintain complete customer satisfaction!' Well isn't that special! I bet nobody ever had that idea before! It's so cutting edge! So .. wow! But really, it is the same policy hookers have and I bet you don't mean the same kind of satisfaction! But just for fun, let's run with that and use it as an example of the difference between real policy and procedures.

Start by thinking about how are you going to maintain customer satisfaction? Hand jobs? Blow jobs? Doggie style? Missionary positions? Anal? What do people like nowadays? What are the latest fuck-fads? What's a good price? In order to keep your customers satisfied you'll have to consistently do some market research with other hookers to see what their customers are asking for, share techniques, etc. Warn each other of high risk customers and lessons learned. Find out what other professionals are charging to keep your prices fair. What about protecting your clients' health? That will help keep them returning customers; you know what they say! A breathing, disease free customer is a return customer! So is there a plan for regular checkups and condom use? Some customers are *only* going to be fully satisfied with some pretty fucked up shit. At what point to you draw the line and say to hell with customer satisfaction! When do you tell your customer, "Get your pony, your gold fish and the fucking spikey thing and get the fuck out!" Do you see how that 'no shit Sherlock' goal turned into a need to define definite course of action and the basis for decisions? It turned into a policy, which needed a clear set of procedures to ensure that the policy was enforced consistently over a long period of time.

What about *NSS policy* to 'It's our policy to source, develop and retain the best Human Capital'? This could also be a policy for the pimps to find new hookers to work them, to lure them, break them in and keep them from running away couldn't it? You see where I am going with this?

Procedures are the step by step instructions on **how** the complete **processes** for an organization to be carried out. They are important for training new employees, making sure everyone in the organization is following the same quality path and consistency is maintained. They are the specific instructions needed to perform a task. Procedures are specific steps in an overall process.

I've found in a lot of companies have policies are all over the place and it gets confusing as hell. They have policies in volumes and yet they still find themselves out of compliance and can't figure out why! It is because they've made it next to impossible to stay within policies. A lot of companies 'fix the problem' by revising the policies, they spend a lot of time and money to revise and organize the policies all the while not having figured out it was the procedures that were really killing them, or rather the lack of procedures. Healthcare providers are very prone to this problem. Let's be honest, procedures are a bitch to write – good procedures are a major bitch to write. They take time, patience, expertise and can only really be done by the highest performers with the most experience in the organization. You can't really have someone outside of the specific organization write them because every company, every organization is unique and the procedures have to suit THAT organization. Hiring a consulting company to come and do it for you is not going to stick. They usually have a set of prepared policies that they may or may not make minor changes to – like add in your company name, and then print. It is a prepackaged product that is almost always a very bad fit. Copy & paste procedures won't serve their purpose. Let me paint you a picture. I have shoes. Horses have shoes. Brakes have shoes. But none of these shoes will work for the other. Simply copying and pasting another company's policies, even a shareholder company's policies, is just another case of horse shoes and brake shoes.

The people you need to write those procedures are the exact people you can't always spare to take the time to write them because they're handling so many other things. That is what makes them experts. Let me just remind you of an old saying, "It takes money to make money". Well that is the same for procedures. It takes time and money, to save time and money. Those high performing experts in your organization should be used for this task so that others in the organization can learn from those high performers, mimic the quality and keep it going. That is what good policies and procedures do – they save you time, money, and out-of compliance headaches in the long run.

People don't mind writing policies so much, they're shorter and faster. You can sometimes copy and paste – SOMETIMES, because policies are general and vague, based on the laws and regulations of the company and standards of the industry. But for the love of all that is good in this world, don't neglect the procedures. If you do, you end up with volumes of rules and regulations, and no shared detail or clarity on how to follow them. Imagine entering a dance competition. The rules say that you must dance the Tango, a dance you've never even seen performed, to specific music you've never hear before, and follow the technical requirements for a version of the Tango you've never learned before; and there are lots of rules about costumes which you've never seen before. There are no contextualized references to make heads or tails out of the policies with. There are a lot of rules on what you cannot do, but no instructions on what you're supposed to do. Of course you're going to be out-of-compliance; you never learned what it is to be in compliance!

The clearest and easiest path forward is that an organization, while keeping their function's approved authority in mind, writes out the **Policy & Procedures (P&Ps)** for the work performed in their own department or organization; starting with the flow chart. Visualize the whole process, step by step and then write it out as though it were a training manual, because it will be. Imagine using it to teach a new employee how to carry out every aspect of business in the organization (department, section, etc.) Laying out the entire instructions as **step by step procedures**; this eventually develops into a complete process. Once that is done, add in the **footnote references** in each step if there are any **policies** or specific **laws and regulations** which govern that particular step or decisions in the processes. Every law, regulation or policy referenced which governs that particular process needs to be included in the **appendices at the end of the process and procedures**.

Development: Policies and Procedures (P&Ps) must be drafted and developed by the actual organizations that are carrying out that work because they are the experts. No other HR or corporate organization should attempt to hijack the development of writing them for other organizations. General rule of thumb…. Stay the fuck out of other people's kitchens. However, once the responsible organization does draft them, they need to be reviewed by legal and sometimes finance organizations before being sent up for approval. The proponent is responsible for the technical aspect of the document, legal is responsible for the legal aspect, your compliance organization should review it for compliance components, and finance does the budget and financial reviews. If you really want to do a good job, have Internal Auditing look at them before they're sent for approval. That's the organization which will be giving you audit items if it isn't done right, so why not get the benefit of their expertise before you launch. You're all on one team anyway; why not play like you are!

Approval: Once these organizations' P&Ps have been completed and properly reviewed by legal and finance they will need to be approved at the appropriate levels. P&Ps that that govern activities for the enterprise including the executive management should be board approved. **APPROVAL Rule-of-thumb:** *You cannot approve the charters, authorities, policies or procedures that define, amend, extend or diminish your own job level, authority, responsibility or liability.* That has to go to the higher powers. It would be the equivalent of employees writing their job descriptions and approval authorities and then telling the management what they have decided as opposed to the management telling the employees.

The Shareholders set the limits for the board's power and responsibilities. The board tells the Officers (C-Suite Executives, General Counsel, and General Auditor) and usually the VPs, senior VPs, general managers or executive directors get their 'powers' delegated from the CEO as long as the CEO has been granted to delegate those specific authorities to the VPs and below. This is usually where many companies get fucking confused! Not just confused, but FUCKING confused. I've seen a lot of CEOs give and take authority, approve policies, make organizational changes which are actually outside of their authority to do so and sometimes go on doing it for long periods until it becomes the norm; even though it shouldn't be. And even worse, is that the Boards don't know any better, fail to notice or give a shit. They just let it go. The **DELEGATION of Authority Rule-of-Thumb** is that if *a specific responsibility or authority* is singled out, spelled out specifically for the Board in the Bylaws or the Articles of Association, it is a responsibility they keep and do not delegate down to the C-Suite executives or below. If approving company policies or the corporate organization is specifically mentioned in

Board authorities and responsibilities, it is one they keep and cannot delegate. Same for the CEO; if a specific responsibility is named for the CEO, the CFO or other Board approved company officers, it is a responsibly that title keeps and doesn't delegate.

The reason for this is, if it is mentioned in the Articles of Association or By Laws, which is a corporate government document filed with the authorities, then whoever is named as a responsible entity will carry the liability if things get fucked up and that doesn't go away even if you delegate the responsibility downwards. Legal accountability or liability can be a bitch! It comes along with the privileges of the chair you sit in. Later I'll explain the '**Standard Corporate Blame formula**'; the bigger the chair, the bigger the % of responsibility you carry when the shit hits the fan. Don't be a gutless weasel and try to sit in the big chair without owning the liability! If you're sitting on a board, and the board is delegated by the shareholders to approve company policies, the board cannot and should not delegate it to CEO Bob; because if CEO Bob fucks up, the board is still liable.

I have actually overheard two board directors having a discussion on this very subject. One was almost bragging how if they delegate all this authority to the CEO, then if something goes wrong the CEO would be responsible, not them. "… if it happens, it's not our signature!" These are the kinds of conversations you love and dread over hearing. Fuck ups!

Annual Review: The P&Ps will need to be stored and accessible by all company employees on an internal company website. If you're a really tiny company you can print them off and put them on a desk I suppose. Save a tree, store them in electronic form. There needs to be someone responsible to ensure that the company's governance and P&Ps are all active, have gone through the proper development and approvals, annual reviews and are all compliant then report that to the board. That would be the Corporate Secretary, or the Policy Manager, etc., just as long as someone responsible is watching the kids.

I have to add here, one of my pet peeves is how easily the word 'policy' is thrown around to describe a practice. Listen! This is for all those stuck up, power hungry office bitches (male or female) that walk around spouting off, "It's against our policy…" pay attention. *First* of all, no one likes you and your shoes are fucking ugly, as is your soul! *Second*, if it isn't actually a written down policy or processes, which has been approved by company executives, then it isn't a fucking policy. Get it? It is annoying as hell to hear "it's against our policy …." or "our policy is…" Really? It's a policy? Can I see it? Can I read it? Can I touch it? Is it posted? Did an executive sign off on it? Can I print off the document and shove it down your damn throat? If not, then it isn't a fucking policy is it?! It's more of a stupid practice which changes according to your whim. And by the way, you sound like a major ass-hole for spouting off rules and practices which aren't actually written down and properly approved as 'policies'. No one may be calling you out on it *to your face,* but everyone who hears you knows that there is no actually policy and you're just an asshole who wants to be pretend to be in charge. NOBODY ACTUALLY BUYS IT! And the other employees do impressions of you when you're not around, "It's our policy…" Sometimes, these 'faux policies' practices can land your ass in court. There is a very good reason P&Ps have to go through so many layers of approvals. A lot of qualified, certified, and authorized people have to make sure that the behavior or actions of the company are compliant.

All this sounds really basic and you may be wondering why I took time to write out the steps of Policy Management 101. Here it comes. You've heard of accountability? It is a word that people sometimes throw around as an excuse to give a presentation about their accomplishments to executive management. The walk through here on governance and policy management basics is to highlight the often missing accountability component which is also key in a compliance program.

What happens if an organization fails to properly develop and maintain their governance? What are their consequences? They should get their asses kicked by the CEO and the board, that's what! And here is how; the Corporate Secretary or Policy Manager, whom ever is responsible for the enterprise policy management and reporting to the board on the issue, includes in their quarterly board report which organizations are operating 'without an approved P&P' or 'outside of their board approved charter'. The board then decides if the signatory or function head of that organization gets to keep his or her signature authority, gets a warning with a limited time of reprieve to get their shit… excuse me… their *ship* in order, or to suspend their signature authority over that organization. That is **policy management accountability**. If the particular manager or function head can't get it together, boot their ass to the curb! They are sucky leaders and horrible managers. These are the kinds of managers that make your good employees leave! Without this policy management and accountability function, boards and executive management can get caught by surprise when concerns turn into serious compliance issues. I've heard it so many times before. A board member or CEO says, "They were doing what??!!" "Why wasn't I told?!" "Who told them they could do it like that??!!" Well, if you don't have a policy management system in place, *you did dumbass*! Silence shows consent! Especially if someone is fucking you over! You gave them approval to do whatever the hell they wanted to do because you didn't enforce a policy management program in your compliance program. You gave the teenager the keys to the car after midnight on a school night! Don't act surprised the police are now on your door step delivering a drunk kid holding your front bumper in their hands.

Governance and P&Ps need to be properly administered with all the checks and balances, or you will end up with is a bunch of siloed organizations self-policing, running amok in their own little kingdoms and not telling the board or shareholders a damn thing! The board will have no damn clue what is going on, until it hits the news or the court room. They cry, "How did this happen???" blaming the company management for the board's failure to do their due diligence and oversight as a board member. Management then blames the bad employees for being out of compliance and the employees blame management for general douche-bagginess and the company is going down the shitter fast. Good employees leave and you're stuck with the schmucks! First people out the door are you best people! Again, organizations *do not self-measure on compliance, performance or accountability.* Managing without measurable oversight is just fucking retarded!

If managers feel the need to blame someone then you can calculate the blame using the **Standard Corporate Blame formula.** (*(Size of salary + Size of chair) / #of people implicated = your % of the blame for the fuck up*).

Regardless of whether or not you were actually there or did anything; inaction or failure to implement the necessary compliance and control measures is the same as shitting on your own floor and inviting other people to do so as well. How do you like being in charge now?

I appreciate the purely diplomatic way pirates chose their leaders. They elect their captain from the best possible candidates they know – one of their own. If their captain screws up, they kill him and elect a new one who will be encouraged not to make the same fucking mistakes. The captain is the one they have to trust to lead and make decisions about their money and welfare. They need to be secure in the knowledge that he's competent. CEO's are the ones the board trusts with shareholders' money and the company's welfare. Unlike a pirate crew, the board doesn't often get to see firsthand the real performance of the CEO or company officers until it's too late. Think about your own company. If the employees were the shareholders and could vote in a CEO and company officers of their choosing from amongst the crew they trust, would it be the same ones sitting in the office now?

7

Reporting Mechanisms

Reporting mechanisms for a compliance program come in several shapes, however no matter what, the primary reporting hotline mechanism for any company will always be the anonymous hotline.

In order of significance there are:

Anonymous

a. Anonymous internet hotlines, which are basically website questionnaire forms you'll fill in and hit a submit button. They provide you an automated 'Report Number' and you'll create a password so that you may actually log in later to check on the status of the report, communicate anonymously with the Compliance Organization if they have any additional questions, etc. This form should not be on your company's server, because that can be traced. You should have the reporting page off of your company's website. Clicking a 'Report an Incident' button or the like, should redirect you to an entirely different web page. It should provide the notice that the reporting is being taken out of the company server to another site to report – to protect their anonymity. These pages should be accessible by smart phone.

b. Toll-free numbers with IVR (International Voice Recognition) to recognize different languages.

Traceable – NEVER to be called Anonymous

    c.   A general email address
    d.   A hotline form *on your company's server*
    e.   Fax
    f.   Postal – snail mail

Walk-in

   o   Reporters should be able to walk into the Compliance organization's office, or into designated company managers to give a formal report and still have their identity protected. This should be formalized in a signed form to allow the compliance professional or manager to keep that reporter's identity confidential and still follow through with a report.

I've seen a lot of companies in the Middle East provide a generalized email as an 'anonymous report' email. *An e-mail address is not anonymous*, even if you call it Hotline@OurCompany.com. Let me say that again. An email address is never, ever, ever going to satisfy the 'anonymous reporting' capability of a company. EVER! E-mails have embedded Domain Name System (DNS), the DNS is one of the most important components of Internet infrastructure. If DNS is unavailable for a site, you can't find resources on the Internet and, likewise, others will be unable to find you. That's because DNS is what translates names such as www.LATimes.com to Internet protocol (IP) addresses such as 199.239.136.855, and vice versa. The DNS is the key to your existence on the Internet. And it is traceable! Tracing e-mails is so easy, anyone can do it. Copy and paste an e-mail header into free websites like IP2Location.com (Yes! That is a real website!) and it will give you the IP address. From there you can locate the sender. Sometimes you can get a name and Google that you'll have a whole history on the person. Now I am not a particularly IT savvy person. In fact, when I got an iPad for my birthday, I had to have my 9 year old turn it on for me, *so if I can figure out how to do this, anyone can.* Your employees know they can be traced and will NOT likely opt to report for fear of retaliation.

Ideally you should provide multiple methods of reporting to make it as easy as possible for reports to be made. In order for you to be considered as having an anonymous reporting system, at least one of the reporting mechanisms must be actually be anonymous. I was asked by an elderly executive once, "Why do we have to make it so easy for the employees to give us problems?" The question honestly stopped me in my tracks for a moment. While thinking through what my carefully worded response would be, the pirate was encouraging me to either just put him out of his misery, or give him a cup of warm milk and a nap. Dinosaur!

There have been a lot of studies done on how long incidents of fraud or embezzlement have been occurring before being discovered by a general audit. They say typically illicit behavior may have been taking place anywhere from 12 to 18 months before it is detected, and even then only 15% of the actual illicit behavior is discovered. I don't think statistics are good here, because the bulk of my experience is in the Middle East and those studies are done in western countries where they actually have an idea of what accountability is, even if the powerful still aren't held accountable. The same studies *I am not going to cite* properly also talk about how much faster incidents are reported, detected and resolved when they are received via an anonymous hotline. But I will say this, if the US and UK are getting those numbers in an environment where people are actually talking about corporate corruption; I shudder to think what those numbers are in this region.

Reporting mechanisms need three things to be successful. The first has to have a truly anonymous capability. The second is a loud, clear and iron-clad 'No Retaliation' policy that is known to be enforced in the company. The third is that if someone is knocking on the door, you better be there to answer. Having a hotline that no one is tending to is careless and screams volumes that your management doesn't give a shit what anyone thinks and fears no consequences. (Yup! The management is flipping the Board of Directors the bird – telling them to 'fuck off!' and the Board is letting them do it!). Lenders, shareholders, employees… might as well know that you are basically giving them the middle finger as well and don't care one bit. You don't care about employee buy-in or trust for the management – so don't be surprised when employees start breaking rules as a habit or leaving the company. You don't care if the complaints fall on deaf ears when suppliers are reporting being asked for bribes in order to be awarded contracts – so don't be surprised when the supplier's name is in the news for bribery and your company is one those listed as having taken a bribe. Your lenders who gave you a lot of money on the condition of your compliance program being FCPA or UKBA compliant might be testing your commitment to that promise by submitting test reports and when they don't get any response – don't be surprised when you get a meeting request from you lenders or turned down if you needed any additional funding.

8

Case Management

Case Management in your company's compliance program is a vital Key Performance Indicator ("KPI") for your compliance organization and needs to be tended to with great care. The processes need to be set up conscientiously. The stakeholders and individuals chosen to be involved in investigations across the enterprise need to be selected carefully. The reporting and auditing functions need to be protected and used for analysis. This is a real life, and valuable tool.

A "case" is any concern or report that is "opened" with a report received from any one of the reporting mechanisms in your compliance program, and then "closed" over a period of time after having achieved a policy defined resolution of the problem, claim, or other complex activity. The report of a concern is received, assigned to the appropriate case manager, inquiries are made and the investigation is handled. The conclusions are formed and recommendations are made for either the Compliance Committee's final decision or the General Counsel, or the President & CEO or the maybe even the Board of Directors – all dependent upon how you defined your Compliance Policy case resolutions. Once a final decision is made and actions taken, the case is then closed. It is likely to involve multiple persons inside and outside of the organization, with varying relationships to each other, as well as multiple documents and messages.

These cases are nearly always automated which significantly removes the risk of human error or misjudgment, or just idiots. Computer software systems are executing tasks and making decisions—the odds are greater that a process completes accurately. These cases must be easy to audit and track the workflows and tasks within the process. The ability to complete all steps of a process more quickly and do so in conformance with the rules that govern it highlight a third benefit of automation: compliance. Most importantly to utilize this process and track-able / auditable data for your accountability is vital.

The Case Management is a valuable analysis tool for the company. You will be able to track what kind of cases are being reported, what organizations or individuals are usually named in these reports, how long are these cases taking to resolve. If you want to know which members of your management or which company policies or practices are driving your good employees away, this is the tool that is like a neon lighted arrow. It will go directly to the source of problems, the king (or queen) asshole, or if you're a positive thinking person and not a pirate – the organization that has the most opportunity for shining improvement. If you receive 20 complaints on the hotline in one month, and 10 of them are HR related and complain about discrimination – you might have some issues on discrimination you need to look into.

The Case Management is literally a 'health diagnostic tool' for your company to understand where the hot spots are, and start looking for resolutions.

9

Investigations, Internal and External

Your compliance policy needs to lay this all out, step by step in a flow chart, and backed up by a Process and Procedures manual. For a couple of very good reasons, *including but not limited to*: (That is a legal-ese 'cover-my-ass' term for a list of things I can think of right now but room for anything else I may have forgotten later on.)

a. Internal Investigation results can sometimes be used against a company or its executives in a court of law. You want to make sure that the chance of them being requested in a discovery motion is as slim to none as possible. Investigation steps, files, records, emails, etc. all need to be processed in a way that can protect them as privilege as much as possible. Does that mean only attorneys can conduct investigations? No. In fact outside attorneys, defense attorneys, prosecution attorneys, etc. all use investigators, paralegals, legal secretaries, and a variety of other staff on investigations and their work is still protected under the Attorney-Client Privilege. This is managed by the way the investigation is conducted and files marked, notes taken and categorized as Attorney Work Product, etc. There are lots of little steps that need to be planned out in your investigation process that will either protect your internal investigations or allow the prosecution to skull-fuck you in the court room.

b. Not investigators are created equally. In a corporate environment you cannot always control or have a say in the individual(s) that will appointed to work with your compliance organization's investigations.

67

You will have people from Security, IT, HR, Finance, etc. and some of them will be really sharp and capable. Some of them are going to be major pricks and the last thing you want to deal with is trying to convince a prick what the steps of the investigation should be. If it is already laid out in a P&P, then the discussion is done. And if the prick doesn't perform, you have a documented reason to get them out of the investigation.

c. Your investigation results may protect the company from liability and provide proof of damages and wrong doing for your company's benefit. If the investigation process is consistent and managed in a concise manner, then your evidence in such cases will be more solid.

Now, let's be clear. When I refer to your company's investigation process I am referring to the policy and procedure that **_all_** of your company's various organizations follow when conducting any internal investigation – same process, same forms, same resolutions, same reporting system, etc. And the process should be cross organizational involvement from legal, auditing, security, personnel, etc. If your company has a different process for different organizations, get your shit together.

Internal vs. External Investigators

If the allegation you are investigating involves a Board member, then find a neutral external investigator to manage it IN ACCORDANCE WITH YOUR COMPANY'S INVESTIGATION PROCESS as possible.

If the allegation you are investigating involves a higher management, a function head, general manager or executive director or company officer, then find a neutral external investigator to manage it IN ACCORDANCE WITH YOUR COMPANY'S INVESTIGATION PROCESS as possible.

If the allegation you're investigating has anything to do with a third party, find a neutral external investigator to manage it IN ACCORDANCE WITH YOUR COMPANY'S INVESTIGATION PROCESS as possible.

10

Program Analysis & Annual Maintenance

Your compliance program and compliance organization should be subject to a greater level of scrutiny and accountability reporting as any other organization in the company. My personal opinion, if you're working in any law related capacity, your shit better be squeaky clean! You better pay more attention to details and scrutinize your organization's behavior more than anyone else's. Otherwise you'll be hypocrites. KPI's for a compliance organization should start with the Case Management trend analysis reports, noted changes to legislation and regulations, annual anonymous employee surveys and exit survey.

Case Management trend analysis reports: It isn't enough to simply show how many cases you managed that quarter or year. You have to show how many reports you received, what types of reports, how many were actionable (should be around 85%), turn-around on reports, and a business analysis report on what you found to be the root causes of those issues. Statistics alone are a lazy ass way of going through the motions of reporting. Provide insight on root causes with sound solutions. This is where you become really unpopular with other organizations because they are going to feel exposed and blamed. Sorry.

Regulatory and legislative Changes: you will need to consistently stay on top of and highlight new laws that will require the company to change their policies, or P&Ps from time to time. You will be required to note when the law was passed, when it will go into effect, and what it will mean for the operations of the company – if anything at all. *Splain' it to them Lucy!*

Annual anonymous employee surveys: Every year your compliance organization needs to send out a company-wide, short, multiple choice, anonymous surveys to gauge how good of a job the company thinks the compliance organization is doing and how good the management is doing. When I say 'the company' I mean everyone. I know sometimes management thinks and acts like they are the company, but the company is actually everyone, including management. Keep it brief, keep it anonymous, and multiple choice. Leave one spot at the end for them to write freely on any specific concern they may have.

Exit Surveys- Don't wait til you have a lot of employees leaving and then hire a consulting firm for an ungodly amount of money to come and give you some half-ass analysis on your employee voluntary

There are basically two methods of calculating your company's attrition rate. First, attrition can be factored out by taking the number of employees leaving for a year, divided by the average total number of employees, multiplied by 100 (in order to give a percentage value). The number of employees leaving and the total number of employees are measured over one calendar year.

$$\left(\frac{NELDY}{(NEBY + NEEY)/2} \right) \times 100$$

Where:

NELDY =   Number of Employees who Left During the Year
NEBY =   Number of Employees at the Beginning of the Year
NEEY =   Number of Employees at the End of the Year

For example, at the start of the year a business had 40 employees, but during the year 9 staff resigned with 2 new hires, thus leaving 33 staff members at the end of the year. Hence this year's turnover is 25%. This is derived from, (9/((40+33)/2))*100 = 25%.

That formula is geared for a manpower study, not an attrition study. Using it for an attrition study is a major cop out and misleading. Let me explain why. If all employees were created equal, and you just wanted to know your manpower numbers and their fluctuations, then use the formula above. However, if you want to know exactly how many people left, and what is making them leave you need to keep it a lot more 'real'.

NEBY – NELDY = YOUR ACTUAL ATTRITION RATE!

When an employee turns in their notice to leave you, you need to provide them with an anonymous exit survey to complete and submit to your compliance organization. It actually might be something that can be resolved and perchance change the employee's mind to stay. But at least each quarter the compliance organization would be able to submit an actual number (%) of people who left which organization and why. It's a beautiful thing this 'transparency' idea! Then, and only then would your really be able to tell if your best people are leaving, from which organization they are jumping like rats off a sinking ship, which member of your management is fucking up, and if there is something salvageable. And you can really be more comparative of what is and how far above or below you are as far as the norm for your company's region and industry. Of course, management is going to hate this idea. They don't like the idea of being made to look bad, especially if they really really are!

What is considered a high turnover rate for your company will depend on your industry and the region of the world you're operating in. In 2006, average turnover rates in the United States varied between around 15 percent annually for durable goods manufacturing employees to as high as 56 percent for the restaurant and hospitality industry, according to Nobscot Corporation. Nobscot is a useful tool and can be accessed for free at:

http://www.nobscot.com/about/turnover_statistics.cfm

The Exit Survey analysis should be much like the Case Management Analysis with a look into which organization is losing its people, what is the reason those people are giving for leaving, and try to identify the root causes and suggest solutions for the CEO, GC and Board to approve of.

11

Supply Chain Management & Third Party Due Diligence

Supply chain management is the oversight of the purchase of materials as they move in a process from supplier to manufacturer to wholesaler to retailer to the company. Supply chain management involves coordinating and integrating these flows both within and among companies. The definitive goal of any effective supply chain management system is to reduce inventory (with the assumption that products are available when needed) and keep costs as low as possible. Some companies use software solutions for successful supply chain management. What we want to address here is the compliance end of supply chain management.

Complex regulatory obligations combined with the still emerging drive of companies towards greater Corporate Social Responsibility (CSR) and sustainability initiatives, along with pressure from customers have driven companies to demand more detailed information from products and suppliers. More detailed information and controls. Consequences from failure to manage these obligations correctly can be catastrophic for the company; going beyond regulatory fines to real business impacts that could mean significant operational losses. Losses from reduced market access and position, or limited competitive agility and decreased customer satisfaction, or you could just end up like the GAP clothing, and be embarrassed as hell when pictures of their manufacturer in Rana Plaza in Bangladesh are shown burned down, leaving over 1,100 dead and countless people injured. Other pictures of other GAP sweatshops emerge showing small Bangladeshi children making children's clothes for GAP. I may be a pirate at heart, but I won't be shopping at the GAP, ever. I boycotted Nike and Apple years ago, as a personal choice. And I've never bought from them again. For companies in the middle, understanding the compliance status and origins of the products, suppliers, and components in your supply chain is a critical aspect of managing your regulatory obligations, communicating to key stakeholders, and mitigating supply chain risk.

Let's be really honest here. Ideally your company will be able to get suppliers and vendors to sign a Supplier's Code of Conduct, and maybe even engage in anti-corruption training. If you can manage those things to happen, then wow, kudos to you. Once you put in a compliance program, it is simple enough to require new vendors and suppliers to sign the Supplier's Code before they are even considered for qualification as an approved vendor. But what about those that have already been approved and you're already doing business with? That is tougher.

In the past I've had clients send out a beautiful hard copy of the Supplier's Code to every one of their approved vendors, business partners, suppliers, contractors, etc. along with a very carefully worded letter that basically says, *'we're implementing a compliance program. We like doing business with you. BUT if you don't accept this gift of a beautiful Suppliers Code of Conduct, sign the enclosed Acknowledgement form and send it back to us, this will be the last contract we sign with you and next year when we review our 'approved vendors' list, you may face disqualification.'* Say all of that in a very diplomatic and professional manner, with a cheer-leader voice on the "Yeah! Compliance!" They need your business more than you need to do business with a company that is afraid to commit to 'no child labor' or anti-corruption clauses.

Sample Supplier's Code of Conduct:

See page 48 for a good example of a Supplier's Code of Conduct.

Third Party Due Diligence

Third party due diligence or "DD" is simply the investigation or audit of a potential business investment, relationship or business partner that any reasonably intelligent and responsible company would do to confirm all material facts in regards to a possible business relationship.

If you were going to contract with a construction company for a multi-million dollar project, you'd want confirmation that the company actually had the technical expertise and manpower to do what you're planning to pay them for. You'd also want to do diligence on their financials to make sure that they had enough capital to cover their expenses while on this project for you; because if they can't cover their manpower costs while on your project then you can smell delays which are going to cost you a lot of money.

There is also the compliance due diligence; checking if this company has been in any legal trouble due to corruption, non-compliance of regulation, court cases or settlements against them or their executives, bad press, etc. This isn't an optional thing people! Engaging in business with someone is just like marriage! Before you even propose you will want to know if that person is married or single, has been married before, abused their last spouse, has kids or other financial obligations, financially stable or in debt, a criminal record, currently wanted by the police, has any diseases, has ever had an STD, etc. If you would do all that for a potential spouse, why in the hell wouldn't you do that for a potential business associate who could cost you hundreds of millions of dollars? A lot of executives don't bother with compliance DD because it just feels like its wasting time, another bit of red tape and some just want to get the contract signed and get going on business. Plus, what the hell do they care if things go bad? It isn't their money that will be lost in the divorce process. It's the shareholders' money. But hey! What's another law suit or investigation from the government or bad press? No problem, right? Wrong! Getting in bed with a filthy whore, and getting press coverage on the event, is a problem. There is a very good reason businessmen and politicians - dirty or clean, do not want to be known associates with convicted criminals; it's bad for the image and bad for business. It's funny; individual executives seem to know this when it comes to their own image and money to be careful, but are very careless when it comes to the company's image. The long and the short of it is, do your damn homework! Know who you're getting in bed with. Don't be stupid and lazy. Stupid and lazy gets into trouble. Imagine the risk of not doing your DD on a potential business associate was the same as getting married without checking the woman out and it was your own dick and your own money at risk. Your dick could end up covered in a blistering rash and fall off, and you could end up too broke to buy the rash cream. Would you do the DD then? Treat your company with the same care you treat your dick and your own money.

Establish the DD criteria, multiple levels of DD (because some bitches just don't need that much investigating, while others need extra), as well as a scoring mechanism to give each potential supplier or business associate a ranking. Establish a company policy that will determine what steps will be taken for suppliers that have a high risk rating but you still want to engage them. By steps, I mean: extra contract clauses you can include in order to protect yourself from liability, would you require them to take anti-corruption training, or is the acknowledgement of the Supplier's Code enough for you? Under what circumstances will a supplier be ranked as a preferred supplier, and which ones will make the 'hell no!' list. How often will you review your approved suppliers list and recertify (prequalify) them? Figure it out; every year, every two years, every three years? The correct answer is... I don't know! Depends how big your list is and how long it would take? If it's a small list, recertify your suppliers annually. If the list is huge, then do it every five years. But for shit sake, do it! Don't be like a sloppy college kid who puts shit in the refrigerator and leaves it there until it becomes a science project. Not recertifying your approved vendors / supplier's list on a regular business is sloppy, dirty, lazy, and means you have a lot of useless crap in your closet. You're obviously not a company that gives a damn about quality or compliance, rules, business optimization; you're unpatriotic, racist and really fucking stupid. Actually I don't know if you're a racist, but I thought I might as well throw that in as well. But if you're not managing your supply chain in your compliance program, you most definitely are stupid.

By the way, if you're one of those who think the Supplier's Code Acknowledgement is enough for every potential supplier, and don't require any further DD, I'll bet you are also the kind of person who doesn't notice when a woman (or man) you just met at a party keeps scratching their crotch like its burning do you? You don't notice, you don't ask - you'd just hit it. And the next week you complain like a fool when you end up at the clinic buying 'special cream'.

Every company needs to define a level of DD for a specific level of contracts. By level of contracts, I mean, how much money is involved. You do not need to do the same level of DD for small contracts as you do for big ones. The risk is not the same, and you need to adjust. I cannot determine the monetary amounts for the classifications, you have to make those determinations yourself because every company is different; big companies can take bigger hits. Smaller companies cannot withstand that much loss so they need to determine their tolerance for risk on how much pain they can afford to take.

The easiest method is to classify your contracts into three categories:

Non-prime contracts: contracts that if you lost money equal to the amount of the contract, you may not even notice; just an 'Awe damn!' moment.

Sub-prime contracts: If you lost the money equal to the amount of the contract, you'd notice, you'd be pissed, but it won't make you lose sleep. Initiate a Level 2 DD, should be sufficient.

Prime Contracts: If you lost the money equal to the amount of the contract, you lose sleep, a lot of sleep. And you are looking over your shoulder every hour because you know someone is going to kick your ass over it. Initiate a Level 2 DD, and if the initial findings raise any flags, then Level 3 DD. However, if the amount is enormous, the contract/agreement affects an area of your company which is critical, then splurge and go for the Level 3 DD right off the bat.

DD Levels:

Level 1, takes anywhere from a few minutes to a couple of days – depending on whether or not you use a DD provider or doing the old fashioned (outdated, time consuming and stupid) way. Level 1 usually includes media and internet searches, English and local language, watch lists, company's financial and legal information, reputation search, etc. I'll outline a general Level 1 DD below.

Level 2: takes anywhere from a week to two weeks. Again, don't do this yourself. It is time consuming, there are tricks to the trade and it is better to pay the fee and have the expert do it. This includes everything in Level 1 and is accompanied by a Business Report, and an overview of a Risk Summary.

Level 3: includes all of the above, with a site visit to the supplier's place of business and an executive summary.

A very general outline of what you can do for a Level 1 DD ranking:

Financial Performance:

1. What is the current year profit (loss)?
2. What is the previous year profit (loss)?
3. What is the current year revenue?
4. What is the previous year revenue?
5. What is the current year gross margin?
6. What is the previous year gross margin?
7. Does the company have pricing power? Why or why not?
8. Criminal fines or civil litigation settlements within the last 5 years?

Country Ethics & Compliance Risk Assessment:

1. Local, regional and country anti-corruption violations?
2. Information from Chamber of Commerce or Better Business Bureau.
3. Other resources?
4. Signatory authorities; owners, shareholders, etc.

International Ethics & Compliance Risk Assessment:

1. Foreign Corrupt Practices Act (FCPA) Allegations / Criminal findings?
2. UK Bribery Act - Allegations or criminal findings?
3. Other Country - Allegations or criminal findings?
4. World Bank Organizations Sanctions?
5. US Office of Foreign Assets Control OFAC Sanctions?
6. Dow Jones Risk & Compliance Rating?
7. International Monetary Fund?

8. Transparency International Perceived Corruption Rating?
9. Politically Exposed Persons List:

Health, Safety & Environmental Compliance

1. OSHA - Occupational Safety Health Administration:
2. Country / Regional Violations (last 10 years)?
3. If applicable, is the research and development program adequately funded?
4. What is the company's reliance on the overall economic conditions?

Anti-Trust & Competition

1. Does the Company have a published Code of Conduct that includes anti-bribery and corruption policies? Does the Company regularly train, and retrain its employees on this policy?
2. Does the Company policy mention fair competition?

Human Capital

1. Does the Company Promote and Practice Equal Opportunity Employment?
2. Does the Company have an established mechanism to receive and handle complaints of discrimination, harassment, unsafe / unhealthy work environments?
3. Is there a human resources strategy that promotes employee development? Employee Training / Development Programs?
4. Does the Company have a published HR policies guide, including employee access to the Saudi Labor Law?

Compliance with Commercial Import / Export Controls (Imports, customs & Duties)

1. Defense Export Controls applicable? (ITAR Compliance)
2. Applicable Boycott Controls?
3. Relationship with sanctioned countries, corporations or individuals?

Media Research:

1. Government & Political Affiliations
2. Legal / criminal
3. Negative Press

This is not an inclusive list. I should have used the Lawyer CMA terminology, *"Level 1 DD includes but is not limited to the list above."*

12

Setting the Tone - Board and Management Training

Let me tell you a true story about setting the wrong tone from the top – and how it ties right in with training your Board and Management.

I was giving a Management Ethics & Compliance Workshop. Now, this is not a workshop to teach executive management about what ethics and compliance are. They should have already been well versed in that by the time they moved to the throne room. This was a workshop the Board directed to be done for all the management in this particular company to teach them about the company's program and their particular role in setting the right tone from the top. It was a good start. But the buck stopped at the next rung of the ladder.

I started the workshop on time and a particular member of the executive management was conspicuously absent. The pirate waits for nobody! I started on time, because that person was not the most important person in the world and I was fucking busy! Ten minutes into the workshop he arrived, walked up to me in the front of the room, and literally shoved the company's Code of Conduct at my face. If I had not jerked my head back, that code would have been up my nose! He said, "I've read this, my comments are inside. I don't need to attend this." Turned on his heel and left as abruptly as he came in. I was shocked. In my head I was pleading with the pirate, '…don't say fuck you! Don't say fuck you! PLEASE DON'T SAY FUCK YOU!' the pirate complied.…. Everyone else in the room was equally shocked; they were literally jaw dropped. Comedy movie quality - jaw dropped!

That was weird fucking behavior. This member of executive management had just joined the company, hadn't even met me before, and had not been involved with the development of the compliance program or the Code - *because he wasn't fucking in the company yet*! Now he was showing up late to a workshop the Board had instructed be done, interrupting it, refusing to participate, making his comments on an already published and printed Code of Conduct, brazenly being a complete asshole in front of his new executive management team! And worst of all, he was also an ugly fucker with really bad breath. Damn! His breath was strong enough to knock a maggot off a gut wagon. Yes, he was close enough I could smell his dog shit breath. The most surprising thing was that my pirate just said, "Not today Satan!" She was not going to be baited *just yet*. Instead she just carried on like nothing had happened, thinking about killing him quietly in the dark; coming out of a shadow to silently make him die eyes wide with fear. She was quiet for that moment, but she got away from me later on.

I need to reiterate here, the point of the workshop was not to teach ethics and compliance to management. If they are in management and needed the basics, we're in a lot more trouble than we think. It was to teach them about THEIR COMPANY'S new ethics and compliance program and how the program works, etc. Including an important section on the how, what and who of internal investigations, what their individual liabilities were, what would happen if they were mentioned in an anonymous report – it goes directly to the Board who would bring in a 3rd party investigation team. That is some considerable risk I thought they'd like to know. The asshole with the bad breath had the agenda prior to the workshop – so he knew what was going to be gone over and still didn't care. Another participant apparently had told the board about the incident. It wasn't me! I swear! He did actually apologize to me in the elevator a couple of days later, and attended the next scheduled workshop with a great deal of dignity and professionalism. It was so disingenuous; what a pussy! Hit a subordinate in the street then apologize in the alley?? That just makes you more of an asshole, a coward and a fake. If you do something wrong to someone else, in front of other people, own up! Nut up! Grab your balls (or your ovaries if you're a woman) and apologize in just as public of a forum as the offense was in. Anything less makes you look like a pussy.

What happened after the asshole's interruption is the point I want to make. The board did their part in directing the workshop take place. He derailed their entire intention and effort within 30 seconds. His abrupt and weird behavior set the negative tone for the rest of the workshop. Nearly everyone in the room was actually interested in the workshop, and genuinely dismayed at the bizarre behavior, except for one particular douche bag. We'll call him Pinhead.

This one manager, not even an executive manager, is rumored to have gotten the job on a project because of 'favors'. Who's your daddy?! So they pawned him off on the project team. He had an influential father, and that was his only redeeming quality. He had no accomplishments he could claim for himself. He was misogynist, unjustifiably arrogant, a blow hard and really ugly from the inside out. He absolutely could not read the faces or body language of people enough to realize when they were getting really, really tired of his constant interruptions or posturing during meetings. I heard people groan in pain if they found out Pinhead was attending a meeting they'd be attending. The dumbass just could not tell that everyone in the room could see right through his complete bullshit and insecurities. I think he actually believed he sounded intelligent when he'd talk. And he didn't. He really didn't.

Pinhead took his cue from the asshole's performance and for three fucking hours just gave me so much shit; heckling me, and literally trying to rally the troops (other participants) to walk out as well. He actually said, "We're managers. We don't need you to tell us about ethics and compliance, right guys?" They just looked at him like they weren't sure if he was joking or really that dumb. He was really *that* dumb. No one was going to follow Pinhead anywhere. Pinhead, was the only lemming in that room – run like the wind! Go! Be free and don't let the door hit you on the way out! No one was going to stop him! He followed that with, *"I worked for JP Morgan, and they only took 19 minutes for their compliance training."* I was so physically and mentally tired at that point; I couldn't hold the pirate in anymore. She came out with a vengeance and it was ugly. With both of my hands down on the table, just short of a slam, before I knew what she was up to, the pirate was leaned in half way across the table from Pinhead, leveled a cold-ass glare straight into his eyes and said; *"Maybe if JP Morgan had spent more than 19 minutes on ethics and compliance training they wouldn't be in the court room right now facing criminal allegations of corruption! If you are that uncomfortable with the subject matter, there's the door!"*[3] [4] [5] I was fighting so hard to stay calm; I was actually shaking in an effort not lurch across that table and rip his stupid face off his skull. The participants on both sides of me rolled their chairs away from me as fast as they could. One told me later that he was sure I was going across that table. That jackass had no idea that I very nearly did. I am ashamed to say, I nearly went O'Ren Ishii! To this day, I am sure he has no idea and if he ever was told, I'm sure just he'd laugh it off as a ridiculous notion that any woman could kick his ass. Every other man in that room knew how close he came to having to go home and explain to his family how a woman kicked his ass in the office. As I said, he could not read people to save his own life. His boss actually came to me later and apologized on his behalf. How lame! His boss had to go apologize for his bad behavior! I asked him why he doesn't do the pinhead a solid favor and guide him! Counsel the dumbass before he burns too many bridges because a lot of people were fed up, especially with his behavior in meetings. He just gave me a look of complete defeat, shook his head and shrugged his shoulders with the most pathetic helpless look I'd ever seen. He was just at a complete loss. I felt so much pity for him. I'd heard from others that even a one hour meeting over a simple issue would be 3 hours of meaningless double talk and imaginary complications if he was there. With me, he took his cue from the Asshole, and ran with it. By the way, that was the closest I'd ever come to losing my cool and breaking the 'no violence' at work rule. Ok, actually the second closest.

[3] Levin, N. (2015) J.P. Morgan Hired Friends, Family of Leaders at 75% of Major Chinese Firms It Took Public in Hong Kong. Wall Street Journal. Nov. 30, 2015. Available at: http://www.wsj.com/ articles/j-p-morgan-hires-were-referred-by-china-ipo-clients-1448910715

[4] Wasay, A. (2016) JPMorgan Chase & Co the Most Corrupt Bank on Wall Street: New Book Claims. Wall Street Journal. Mar 18, 2016. Available at: http://www. bidnessetc.com/65731-jpmorgan-chase-corrupt-bank-wall-street-book-claims/

[5] Eskow, R. (2014) JPMorgan Chase's $13 Billion Shadow. Wall Street Journal. August 15, 2014. Available at: http://billmoyers.com/2014/08/15/ jpmorgan-chase%E2%80%99s-13-billion-shadow/

Back to the point; there were three parties to blame in that situation. Can you guess who they are? The first two are kind of obvious.

1) Asshole, who was acting like an ugly Richard Cranium and didn't value the subject matter, professionalism, respect or even manners; or
2) Pinhead who took his cue from Asshole – because he selected the bad behavior of Asshole to model. I told you, he is stupid! You cannot fix stupid!
3) And the third?

Nope! Not me! The third one is not me! In fact, if it was you in that situation; I challenge you that you wouldn't have clocked him, repeatedly, happily and gleefully. The fact that he walked out with all of his teeth, speaks volumes to my self-control. I swear to you my body was replaying every muscle memory of every fist fight I'd ever been in since 2nd grade when I kicked Larry Cooper in the nuts on the playground for kicking me in the shins with his new cowboy boots. My body was on complete autopilot overload; compelling forward me tear the skin off his neanderthalic skull. To be honest, that is an alarming sensation to have to fight your own flesh for control of your actions. I deserved a fucking gold star of self-control!

The third party to blame was ***every other participant in the room who had chosen to remain silent during the meeting*** while Asshole and Pinhead tanked a 3-hour workshop that took six months to prepare. Why was it their responsibility to say anything? I am glad you asked that! Actually, I don't care if you did or not, because I am going to tell you anyway. Because they were all managers and executive management! It was their responsibility to do the right thing. To set the tone from the top even if the head of the organization is a dick who has an army of pinheads supporting him. If you are a supervisor, manager, executive manager, or board member you are responsible! You get paid more, to do more, to work more, to take more, to risk more *and to be blamed more*. That is how it works. Even if you're the only one with any sense in the company, even if it's risky to speak up, especially if it's risky to speak up! That is what it means to be in management. If you don't like it, don't take the fucking job or salary.

Every participant in that room understood the behavior was wrong. They all understood Pinhead was modeling bad behavior, yet NONE of them spoke up against it during the meeting when it was crucial to speak up. They just sat there and watched it happen, but they felt bad about their silence. I know they did because they all talked to me one by one after the workshop to share their personal dismay and disgust at the events.

It was a nice gesture, but didn't do anyone any good. When I needed wolves, they were sheep. The most hurtful thing is the silence of friends and allies, not the words of enemies. There was a time, before I became a pirate, that the silence of friends and allies while I suffered would cause me so much pain, I would be in tears before I could get all the way out of the door of a conference room. Seedy management can be so cruel. They can damage your reputation, your career, your health and your sanity if you let them; and especially if you're standing alone. You can withstand anything they can dish out if you only could rely on other managers speaking up when they see such things and keeping their own in check.

Companies can lose some of the best brains in their organizations to the abuse of assholes and silence of sheep. Why do you think I became a pirate? There was no one willing to speak up, to protect me or others. Even though so many around me professed to sympathize and say things like, 'you didn't deserve that' or 'I hate to see them do that to you'. Talk is cheap. A very dark voice inside of me started to wake up and one day I didn't hope for the assistance of sheep any more. I made a decision. If anyone wants to throw me to the wolves, I'll come back leading the pack. Their silence didn't hurt me anymore, it disgusted me. Fuck those sheep – not literally. Fuck cowards – not literally on that one either. I only need the pirate. Nothing pisses the pirate off more or looks more cowardly than sheep. If a member of management complains and whimpers there is too much corruption or bad politics my answer is and, 'So what are you doing to fix it?" Aren't you also in management?' Any sheepish excuses only make me think, "Then you're no good to the company. Sheep add no value." They'll take the salary and the authority of a management role, but avoid the risks and responsibilities at any cost! Shit or get off the pot! In the sheep's defense, sometimes they just don't realize the affect they have in silence. Naw! Never mind. Sheep have no defense for being useless.

Management and Boards don't necessarily need workshops to train them on what ethics and compliance are; they need workshops to remind them what role they play setting the right tone from the top in the company in order to incorporate them into the company's culture. They need this training to tell them where their liabilities are and remind themselves that the bigger the chair, the bigger the job and the bigger the responsibility.

In addition to the Tone from the Top training, your management and board should have training on an annual basis on risk areas specific to your company by compliance or legal professionals. The reality is that no matter how skilled and informed a manager or board member may be, they may not actually be legal and compliance experts – even though they usually think they are regardless. Unless you're talking about the General Counsel, and even the GC needs training on setting the tone from the top. It isn't a legal or regulatory issue that needs to be addressed; it's an organizational and individual behavior issue that needs to be understood. Putting solely lawyers or auditors in charge of compliance training is like putting a computer engineer in charge of in-patient psychiatric care. They may be fantastic engineers, but psychiatry is just not their field of expertise. There are a lot of assholes, and even more pinheads to follow them, but the silent masses out number them all. If even ONE of those other participants had spoken up with an assertive tone and put Pinhead in his place, the tone would have been set to promote the right message. The right message being, *'This matters! It is important to us all'*.

Shoving the Code of Conduct in your Compliance professional's face, making dismissive comments about 'the rules' in meetings, making crass water cooler comments about the Security Manager's secretary's ass are all setting a negative tone from the top. You're in management; you get paid more to tolerate more, to risk more, to do more, and to show more. Management often complains that no one listens to them. But in reality your employees are always watching and always listening. They hear you, but may seem to be ignoring you because you're an asshole. But make no mistake; they do pay the closest attention especially when you don't want them to. They listen even when they are trying not to. They listen and absorb the behavior. And they repeat the behavior. That is how institutionalization starts. This is how new employees join a company, and adapt to the corporate culture, whatever that culture is that has been established at the top and rolled down.

Institutionalization is the process which translates an organization's *actual values* – not the values you put on posters and 'feel good' emails but the actual values you've practiced, into the daily activities of all of its employees. It is the adaptation of new employees to the organization's 'normal' behavior. It integrates the fundamental values and objectives into the organization's culture and structure.

Let me break this down in a way that I hope will shock you into the reality of it. Let's compare how institutionalization works with a company to how it works in prison or mental asylums.

CORPORATIONS	PRISONS / ASYLUMS
Depersonalized from the beginning	
Good: Getting the department or organization of the new employee involved immediately in their onboarding process. Bringing them on board with a strong 'welcome! You're part of OUR team' will help them quickly identify with a group for comfort and support. Acceptance into the flock of their new chosen few. Making sure their work stations is ready as though they have been expected with great anticipation. Keep the Code on the desk in plain sight. Stepford wives of the corporate world.	The process of denying the person their own identity starts when the inmate or patient enters the door, then are weighed, photographed, fingerprinted, bathed, had all personal possessions removed, and are forced to dress in uniforms.
Bad: Assigning the newly hired an employee a company ID number and badge, relying on a badge number not a name to identify them. Making them feel very much like the 'new kid in class' when bringing them to their department or organization without a proper welcome or even a ready work station. Categorizing them by status, ranking, grade code, etc. ignoring their human qualities. Photographing, fingerprinting, etc. Enforcing a strict dress code. Showing them a desk and chair then walking away.	

Force a break with the outer world

Good: For 8 to 10 hours a day, you have this person who should be welcomed by new friends and team mates they never imagined could exist. A team that will want to be introduced to them, and will want to know all about their history and experience in the introductions, and a team that will help them excel at their job. Making a new employee think that they just hit the co-worker jack pot and happen to land in the best department in the company will be almost memorizing. A world that literally beckons them to 'Come forth and enter'... it won't be what most people expect and they'll come. They'll join, because whatever negative thing there was that made them leave their last job – this welcoming support will be a cure that ails them. (Incidentally... it is possible to find this. I speak from experience.)

Bad: Dropping them into a new department with strangers (we'll call them co-workers) who may or may not be happy that they are there, for 8 or more hours every day. The pressure new employees will face in trying to win the approval and acceptance in their new environment – a forced focus that takes their attention

Forced physical separation from the external world and denying them visitors forces them to face into the institution rather than concentrate or long for external contact. Allowing visitors only as a reward for acceptance of institutional rules is a method of NLP. After a visit from family, inmates or patients are watched carefully to see how they behave. They know they are under greater scrutiny so they feel the stress of needing to be extra good, extra careful to avoid showing any outward signs of rejection of the institution.

completely from the outside world and makes 'work' their new universe. Employees are usually placed on an initial probationary period (usually 90 days) in which they can be terminated without cause. The 90-day period of heightened emotional stress opens the employee to greater suggestibility and makes the adaptation more subtle.

CORPORATIONS

Forced Obedience

Good: A no nonsense approach isn't really difficult to figure out, but can be surprisingly hard to stick to. When the company adopts a *'companies are good, only people are bad and if you're bad this company will spit you out immediately'* attitude it will work! From the beginning new employees **OF ALL LEVELS WORKERS AND LEADERS ALIKE** will be told there is no tolerance for intentional, negligent (lazy ass) or illicit behavior and hear the stories of even executives who were fired for it, the stories will stick. (Especially if they're true.) Stories are how we institutionalize for everything – religious stories of prophets and sinners, social group gossip about sluts and saints' punishment and redemptions, corporate stories of fraud and whistleblowing. And the checks and balances of authority and power are laid out, visible and in USE!

PRISONS / ASYLUMS

Unquestioning obedience is forced by harsh punishment, both psychological and physical. The person may be required to 'willingly' engage in humiliating acts. There may be deliberate 'will-breaking' activities, typically as part of the 'welcoming' initiation rites.

Bad: In corporations, this comes in the form of psychological manipulations. This can be accomplished by either fear of punishment or the risk of being seen in a negative light. Either way, the emotion is real and that creates a chemical brain environment open to suggestion. These suggestions can be detrimental and if management thinks they can control what goes in once that door is open, they're fucking stupid.

A note on emotional manipulation - when an employee dares to speak up or speak out, and some idiot supervisor or managers tries to get them to shut up and go quietly back to their desk by saying things like, *"We heard bad things about you, but I ignored them and hired you anyways".* They might as well just say, *"Nobody likes you, and I am your only friend. So be submissive and grateful to my every whim because you owe me. No complaining while I fuck you over, cause that's what I'm into!"* Trying to humiliate the employee with a threat from an unseen, menacing force who is anonymously complaining about them while simultaneously trying to make them feel indebted for giving them this miraculous chance that somehow they might not actually deserve. That is really a **bullshit coward move!** And if you're hearing this kind of bullshit from a supervisor or manager, just know if they had actually heard bad things, they wouldn't have hired you. Corporations are not charitable organizations and they wouldn't have hired you unless they thought they could use you or you're related to someone they need something from. And to the assholes who try to use this tactic; Fuck off! You're pathetic!

CORPORATIONS	PRISONS / ASYLUMS

Destruction of Self-Determination

Good: Self-determination is only bad in a company when people start to act outside of their authority, which can put a company at risk. To keep this in check, make sure that employees know the right way to communicate up and out of the company. Make sure that approval authorities are clear, easily accessible to know. Draw the lanes very clearly and give clear signs where people can go and not go; keeping in mind not to restrict to the point that employees feel they have no buy-in. It is a difficult balance, but it is achievable.

Bad: When the company's policy or practices allows or fails to prevent management from making unilateral decisions on a whim without the necessary checks and balances. When new employees join a company and feel as though they are trapped, there is no control or influence over their own careers, and it is more like the wild, wild west than a corporation.

Forcing obedience acts to destroy self-determination. This may be continued to the point where the inmate does not even know who he or she is. Attacking them with verbal abuse continues to erode their sense of an integrated self. Giving them menial tasks below their usual professional level show them as inferior. A simple and powerful method is to deny them even their name, reducing them to a number. Everything that they possess, even bedding, may be regularly changed, so they cannot even form attachments to inanimate objects.

Even pirate ships need a captain, so it is expected and accepted that management needs to control the company in order for it to thrive, and employee behavior is part of that. But that need to control can go from a healthy corporate culture of ethics and compliance with appropriate controls, checks and balances to a psychologically destructive environment where management oversteps on the wrong controls, and is vacant on the right ones. Behavior is modeled and mimicked as a survival mechanism; if the leaders are modeling bad behavior then that is what is going to be mimicked across the organization. (Even if the management is not aware that their behavior is bad, *and they never do*.) The process of institutionalization is complete when the employee fears and rejects any change to the status quo – even when the status quo is destructive. Or when employees believe that any improvement to the corporate culture – albeit desirable, would be impossible to achieve they have been fully assimilated and management has killed them.

When management actively and/or unconscientiously conveys hopelessness to employees and each other, employees absorbs it. Eventually good employees with options leaving the company – literally seeking sanctuary, leaving only those employees who gave up (disengaged) to carry on and perpetuate the negative corporate culture.

So, management (actually talking to the Board here…)! Make a decision, and there are only two choices! You either promote ethics and compliance on a daily basis – just like safety and loss prevention; actively setting the right tone, or stay silent and let the pinheads and assholes set the tone. Doing nothing makes you sheep, not management.

13

Employee Training & Awareness Programs

Don't expect anyone to do anything right without having first taught them how to do it. Even the most basic of functions have to be taught right, if you're going to do it right. If you want your kids to crap in the toilet and not on the floor or in their pants, you have to potty train them. You have to teach them the rules. Likewise, if you want your employees to make the right decisions, you have to show them what the right decisions are and where to go if you have questions. This starts with your employees' on-boarding and orientation and continues throughout their employment with the company with training and awareness programs to keep the subject at the forefront of their minds while engaged in activities on behalf of your company and your management.

If your company's new employee on-boarding process amounts to, "Here's your ID and your desk… best of luck! We'll let you know when you fuck up.", well you can't really complain if they fuck up… because you just set them up for it. I mean, you'll complain, but you shouldn't because the fuck up started with you.

New employee on boarding

A company is a living, breathing organism. An organism is any complex thing or system having properties and functions determined not only by the properties and relations of its *individual parts*, but by the character of the whole that they compose and by the relations of the parts to the whole. Companies are made up of different individual parts, each with its own function and ways of interacting with each other. It grows, it changes, and it behaves. There is a consciousness and directive in every company. When a new employee joins that company, they quickly begin to assimilate that consciousness and assume the motivations as their own. Also, obvious or not, new employees can introduce changes to the company as well. Their past experiences, personalities, drives, expertise and even their likability can have an impact on the corporate culture like the domino effect.

You have the choice of letting the company take on a life of its own with no well thought out direction - this would be the equivalent of sleep walking in a mine field. Or you can design your own corporate culture and make the proactive decision that all current and new employees will be assimilated into the culture that YOU picked.

On-board your employees with a *quality* orientation with the Employee Handbook and Code of Conduct central to that training. Teach them about the company, its business, the personnel processes which they can reach out to for assistance, etc. All tied in and detailed in your Employee Handbook. But remember to leave a special time for your ethics and compliance orientation. Give them a desk top copy of the Code to keep on their desks at all times. Well in sight, well in mind. Lay it out clearly in the on-boarding orientation; here are the rules, here is what we consider breaking the rules, here is how we expect you to follow the rules, here is where you can go to have your questions or concerns answered safely, and this is what is going to happen if you fuck up. Don't do half-ass job on-boarding regular employees and then bend over backwards for new employees in management. It really sends the wrong message; that regular people – like 90% of your company, don't matter a fucking bit!

You will get what you train for. If you don't train for ethical and compliant behavior… you will not get it. YOU WILL GET WHAT YOU TRAIN FOR.

Ethics and Compliance Training

Different functions have different risks. Just as different levels of responsibility in a company carry different and greater risks. The higher you go, the farther you have to fall. Your Finance organization is not very likely to risk discrimination charges in their hiring practices, but HR will. And your HR isn't likely to be able to embezzle as easily as someone in Finance. Design your compliance training to be directed towards the level and function risk related to each organization. Training can be either in class or e-learning. Making it easy to get assigned, done, tracked and reported –translates to learning management software. There are plenty of good companies out there; Click 4 Compliance, Corpedia, Network, etc. You pick one that fits your budget and needs. And get the annual course for your recertification based from your own Code customized if you are a mid to large sized company. You'll use it the most and it is better than having to pay for the license every year. I found C4C my personal favorite.

You can even arrange anti-corruption training to your suppliers. Yes they will be a little resentful and resist. But as long as they don't have to pay for it, it can be tolerable. Remember, you're the customer and the customer is always right. Just dig your heals in and stand firm so they understand resistance is futile if you make it so. They want your business. You want less liability. Take the training or be discarded – they will make the right choice.

Yearly recertification

When an employee is on-boarded properly, their new hire employee orientation and the compliance orientation should count for their first year's compliance certification. On the anniversary of their hire date, they should be given a refresher course via e-learning from their desk, coupled with an affidavit of conflict of interest.

Monthly awareness program themes

Awareness programs are meant to get people's attention, be informative, and so fucking memorable that you will not be able to forget whatever the theme was that month. Just like television commercials that stick in your head! "Plop plop fizz fizz.. oh what a relief it is!" for the American readers, and for the Middle Eastern readers, "*Mafi Danou*!?!?"

This means a new theme every month, talking points in communication meetings, eye catching and funny e-mail messages or videos. If it is at all possible, go for the humor. Work is such a drag for so many on a day to day basis. People don't remember what you said; they remember how you made them feel. And if you can attach a strong feeling of humor and relief in an otherwise bleak or stressful week – to a compliance theme everyone is overly sensitive talking about openly - it is going to be positive and memorable. It will be talked about. It will be appreciated. It will get the message through.

My absolute favorite of these come from Corpedia' s Second City – RealBiz Shorts. They are witty, funny, take a generally boring subject and make it memorable. You can make promotional incentive programs each month based on their business shorts. The idea is to teach, and keep it repeating in their heads – and still keep it interesting enough the employees won't want to intentionally mentally block it from their conscious mind. Get your employees talking about the elephants in the building. You want them to talk about what your compliance theme is for that month as much as they talk about the last episode of Black Sails, Vikings, American Horror Story or Game of Thrones.

14

Incentive Programs

It is widely believed and repeated, that incentives can help drive behavior in any organization; whether it is a school, company or just getting your kids to do their homework and chores – at least that has been the school of thought for about the last couple decades.

The use of incentives in the context of compliance programs has been really slow to catch on as a normal part of the program. I think this is due in part because while many CCO s may understand how to weave them into a compliance program to direct good behavior, their management doesn't understand that "appropriate incentives" are a helpful element of an effective compliance program. The failure of some of compliance professionals is to sufficiently explain the benefits and ease at which they can be utilized. I include myself in that failure. I have yet to be successful at getting the message of positive and negative reinforcement for compliance programs to any of my clients. Selling their value is not my strong suit. You can quote as many authorities as you want, but unless you can 'sell' it to management in a small, candy coated pill that won't cost them much or better yet, anything at all, then incentive programs are hard to get in. *That's what he said*. It's hard enough to get executives to put in a compliance program, now you want them to pay employees extra or give some reward or benefit when employees do what they're supposed to do anyway? Comply? Silly compliance person! What were you thinking?

On the flip side, in my experience, when the incentives have gotten in they work as positive reinforcement *for the very short term*, but in the long run not so much. I've seen incentive rewards succeed at securing one thing only, temporary compliance. Once the rewards run out, people revert to their old behaviors. I think the same is for punishments; once the fear is even slightly out of mind the behavior reverts back to what it was before.

To be clear, I think incentives are nice. Who wouldn't like a little extra 'something' for being good boys and girls? But I am not really sold on the idea that they so very effective. I haven't seen incentives make any lasting change in individual or group behavior. I realize there have been a lot of studies that say they do, but from what I've observed, they don't stick. I find them, along with punitive measures which are sometimes enforced and sometimes not, to more of an obvious manipulation. Most university graduates know about Skinner's rats, and while we may call it the 'rat race', we shouldn't presume that employees can be so easily manipulated like rats in hot-wired boxes. I am not opposed to trying Skinner's methods on some of the management I've worked with in the last two decades. I don't even need them to be learning anything. I just like the idea of putting arrogant, abusive, evil assholes in hotwired metal cages and subjecting them to repeated electric shocks. Welcome to the dark side. The humor maybe disturbing, but we have better cookies.

The message manipulative management needs to take away from this is not to presume you can get anything over on your employees with psychological or emotional manipulation because you're **so** much smarter and they're all dumb. I've seen this so many times it just makes me laugh because *it isn't funny*. Business plans and man-power reports talk about sourcing, hiring and retaining the "best and the brightest employees"; then once the employees are hired something unexplainable happens. They become dim witted imbeciles in the eyes of management. The management treats them like idiots who can and must be bullied into submission. Management becomes Col. Jessep in the final courtroom scene with Jack Nicholson and Tom Cruise in 'A Few Good Men'.

Nicholson: "You want answers?"

Cruise: "I think I'm entitled to it."

Nicholson: "You want answers?!"

Cruise: "I want the truth!"

Nicholson: "You can't handle the truth!"

Nicholson's character, Coronel Jessep is arrested and stands trial for conspiracy and murder right after that. It was one of those movie moments where the whole audiences are just ready to come out of their chair and scream "HA! Take that motherfucker!" at Jessep (Nicholson). We all love it when the little guy gets justice, because we have all felt bullied at times. Cruise handled the truth right down to Jessep's ass going to prison! To speak frankly, when management talks or acts as though their employees are stupid and can't handle the 'truth' of complicated matters, it is actually a reflection on management, not the employees. You either hired idiots or you're the idiots for under estimating them. Either way, treating your employees as though they are incompetent and couldn't wrap their brains around the kinds of complicated matters management is burdened with will back fire on management every single time.

Which kind of leaves us back at square one – how do you change or guide the behavior in a company to a culture of ethics and compliance. I think you need to go back to what I wrote about management & board training, and institutionalization. Chose the positive 'institutionalization', and you'll be able to figure it out just fine.

Treat your employees like the intelligent professionals you wanted to hire, give them the tools and development they need, and simply make your compliance requirements a matter of fact – '*Take care of our company in this manner, do your job in this way or get the fuck out of the company!*' It doesn't matter how big your chair is. The Society of Corporate Compliance and Ethics has a publication on Incentive Programs for compliance programs. I recommend reading it for more information. I'm not going to give you the link here. That would take away the incentive to get that great feeling of satisfaction you'll have when you find it on your own – so it won't mean as much to you. How is the incentive working so far? You gonna go look for it or just move on?

15

Dash Board Reporting

Monthly and quarterly dash board reporting to your management and board are excellent tools to show them the health and hotspots in the company. It leaves out the confidential details of the individual compliance reports and investigations, but allows them to get a feel for what is going on with real time information. These dashboard stats are very useful and significant in your compliance organization's annual accountability report. How many reports are being made? Is the number of reports going up or down? What types of reports are coming in? How long are they taking to resolve? What types of resolutions are being made? What are the root-causes for the concerns being reported; bad policies, sucky managers, discrimination, safety violations, fraud, harassment, corrupt corporate culture? You cannot correct what you cannot measure! You cannot measure what you cannot see! If you're relying on one person or organization to provide that information without the safety back up of an automated system, you're an idiot. The dash board reports are usually automatically available from your case management system. If not, you have a bad system. They need to be easy to read, short, real-time user interfaces, showing a graphical presentation of the current status and trends of your company's compliance key performance indicators to enable instantaneous information and a direction on where to dig deeper for explanations from management.

However nice all those things I just mentioned are, the real reason I am a huge fan of those month, quarterly and annual dashboard reports is for accountability.

It puts a lot of pressure on your compliance team, other organizations in the company that involved in investigations, and management. Having a truly anonymous reporting system, a case management system to track the progress of those reports and the dash board reports to top it off are a fantastic way of really being transparent with the Board. It's like suddenly turning the lights on and catching the mice and roaches partying in the middle of the room before they scurry and hide. Employees will have to be on the straight and narrow (well, narrower than they would be without it) because everyone has the ability to voice their concerns about operations. Every employee in the company will have become walking, talking security cameras and listening devices.

If there is a toxic organization or manager within the company, your attrition rates and incident reporting statistics on the dash board for that area will show a hotspot that needs to be looked into. If the compliance organization or compliance committee – or whoever the hell you have doing investigations, is doing a good job, it will show. If they're not, and reports are not being responded to, cases are being held open too long, etc. it will all show up on those dash board reports. And then if the board is awake and not retarded, *'Lucy you got some 'splaining to do!'*. Good employees and qualified management welcome scrutiny into their work and organizations. You propose a system like this and the ones who have nothing to hide will welcome it with open arms. Because they are smart enough to know you cannot reward what you cannot see and measure. Likewise, slacker employees and shady management absolutely don't want anonymous reporting, a case tracking system and they certainly do not want a dash board report which could possibly contain negative information about them or their organizations presented to the board. Cockroaches and rats love the dark.

They will give any excuse why company either doesn't need or doesn't want it. And sometimes they can be convincing. They kinda have to be. Their career and sometimes their freedom from incarceration is on the line. They know… Bubba be waiting on bitch to arrive!

To be honest, I don't think prison is really a factor in their fear of exposure in this region. It should be, but it isn't. I think the fear is to their reputational damage for themselves and their families. Once there is a genuine threat of getting caught, it becomes almost an epic battle to 'protect their family'. What never seems to sink in is that their own actions and illicit behavior are what put their reputation and family at risk in the first place.

16

Self-Disclosure – To Disclose or not to Disclose? that is the question

If a crime is committed in your house, like a murder during a dinner party, do you call the police? Let's say you look over at the piano and Joe, who was the life of the party an hour ago, is literally dead at the keys. Do you think to yourself, 'Hmmm, I am not sure how he died but, this will look bad and it may affect my property value if people knew about it. I'd better put Joe in a hole in the back yard.'

Remember, there is a party going on and others have already noticed Joe isn't playing with as much enthusiasm as he was an hour ago. Now I know this is silly, but some companies actually go through this same thought process. There is a crime committed on the premises, a crime of corruption. People in the company are aware of the incident. There is evidence – a 'body of crime'. And chances are pretty damn good that more than one person knows exactly how it happened and who did it. The odds of at least one of the people who have knowledge on the matter not having been involved in the actual perpetration of the crime are pretty fucking good. The odds of that person or someone that person talked to reporting you to the authorities or in the least spreading the story around the company are even better! Your compliance policy needs to have a very clear plan and description of what types of incidents your company is required to report on, and when. I could put a list down here, but no matter what I put it would be wrong somewhere in the world. This is the part where the lawyers come in really handy. Depending on where you are, what kind of industry you're in, what occurred, etc. You should have an established path forward for what you need to report to the authorities and when you don't need to. Keep in mind there may be penalties for not reporting certain things, and if it is a criminal act.. be very very careful. Self-reporting potential violations to authorities can reduce significantly the negative consequences that may otherwise flow from compliance lapses.

This is one of those instances when you want to look for 'best practices' standards. And let me be clear. The standards of best practices for anti-corruption compliance are not set by consultants or overpriced law firms. They are set by the law enforcement organizations that will put your fucking ass in jail for breaking the rules. They don't always make it easy and just 'spell it out' for you. You have to actually pay attention to the news. What companies are getting their asses in trouble for, which executives got caught and are on their way to the Bendover Hotel, how much is being taken away in fines, were there discounts or time off for good behavior, and how did these suckers get caught. CASE DETAILS MATTER A WHOLE FUCKING LOT! Read them! They aren't just 'something that happened to someone else'. It is something that can happen to your company and your executives as well. Do you know what we call an executive who didn't pay attention to headlines and case studies? Inmate No. 484673 or Bubba's Bitch. We can learn a lot by watching other people's mistakes. Sometimes what 'not' to do is the best lesson. This is where we can get some good insight for our own internal compliance policies and procedures. Is the company using some of the same techniques and practices as those companies who got caught? Is your management still in the 'we won't get caught' loser mentality?

In regards to self-disclosure, the best source for 'best practices' in anti-corruption compliance is the law enforcement agency that has shown the biggest teeth, longest reach, and most aggressive disposition in regards to corruption. That would be the US Department of Justice ("DOJ") and the Security Exchange Commission ("SEC"). They are the two government entities that have joined forces like the Wonder Twins to fight corruption outside of US boarders using the magic powers of the FCPA. In numerous conferences, articles, interviews and publications the DOJ and SEC have repeated the same themes; that companies need to have effective compliance programs and a proper self-disclosure policy when a compliance violation is identified. They have *reiterated* the value of cooperation during an investigation, which I will go more into that later. It always amazes me no matter how many times they repeat these things, executives ignore them. You know what they call management that habitually ignores laws, regulations and government authorities in any country? Fuck ups. Inmates. Unemployed. Divorced. They have lots of names, and some carry more than one. They must have selective hearing. When they talk openly in the news about governments working together, do we not realize that means they are sharing information with other governments? And we know governments don't work together unless they're getting something out of it. The DOJ and SEC will share NSA gathered information about you to other governments! No matter where you are in the world. The NSA is the US government organization that will to spy on whomever the fuck they want. The DOJ and SEC have made it very public and matter-of- fact that foreign corporations should expect that their executives are being watched and listened to. Do you think because you're in the Middle East, Europe, Africa or Asia you're out of reach? You think that the NSA wouldn't find anything a foreign executive has to say on his personal phone, private email, work phone or email useful? We need to pay attention when the most successful spying organization in the world gets in bed with the most successful law enforcement agencies in the world, because their pillow talk is about companies and executives outside of the US and how to fuck them up.

Well, executives may just react to these warning by resolving not to talk openly or take extra precautions about their communication, and they should. But here is another important thing to keep in mind. Remember all those people at the party that saw dead Joe at the piano. They do talk. They talk on the phone. They talk in emails - work and personal, they chat on their iPhones and iPads. They talk about you, your house and dead Joe. And everyone EXCEPT the company's management who wrote them off as too dumb to notice the dead guy at the piano is listening closely to them. Can you spell N.S.A? What management thinks of as secrets kept safely within their walls, are not secrets at all. Don't take my word for it. Just Google "NSA FCPA", and see for yourself. I fucking dare you! Companies are not going to succeed in hiding anything, and all they will do is piss off the enforcing agencies for not only failing to disclose, but attempting to cover.

Don't take my word for it! Let me give you an example of the benefits of self-disclosure. **PetroTiger** promptly made a full disclosure and cooperated with the DOJ regarding a scheme some of its executives had to bribe government officials in Colombia. As a result (reward) for their disclosure and cooperation no charges were filed against the company. However, two executives ended up pleading guilty to both money laundering charges and FCPA violations, and a third was charged. Here is the reason I think executives don't want a self-disclosure policy written into their compliance program. While it will be good for the company, it allows executives to be more exposed and individually accountability. Just like the PetroTiger executives. That company's shareholders stuck to its compliance program policy of self-disclosure and limited its liability and those executives got exactly what they deserve – held accountable. Justice baby! As a compliance professional, that is what I like to see. Protect the company, and punish the bad apples. Corporations aren't evil. The mother fuckers running them are. They are the cancerous cells in the organism and I am all for cutting out the cancer.

In another example, Japan's **Marubeni Corporation** paid US $88 m and pled guilty 8 FCPA charges, and admitting it bribed Indonesian officials to win an electricity contract for itself and a partner, Alstom SA. Alstrom is always in trouble for this shit – Indonesia, Egypt, Saudi…. Marubeni initially refused to cooperate with the DOJ's investigation. This wasn't Marubeni's first trip to the principal's office either. In 2012, Marubeni paid a $54.6 million criminal penalty to resolve FCPA charges for its role as an agent of the KBR-led TSKJ Nigeria joint venture. It was charged in that case with conspiracy to violate the FCPA and aiding and abetting. It received a two-year deferred prosecution agreement that ended on February 2014. If Marubeni had self-disclosed and cooperated the second time around, the US $88 m the sentencing guideline would have lowered their fine by 58%.

SECTION III

Health Checking

17

Shitty Governance

One of the reasons governance is hard to get right, is because everyone knows exactly what it is, and no one seems to know the same thing. Have you ever been in a meeting about governance and just looked around the room, listening to the discussion which has completely gone off track and wondered, 'what the fuck are they talking about?' - so many 'know-it-alls' who know completely different shit. It baffles me every time how things can so easily go so horribly off track. The conversation would start out pretty good, participants seemed confident in that they had something to offer on the subject. But then they would get into other shit; goals, mission and vision statements, processes, etc. All these things are *related* to actual governance, but are not actually governance.

So I think before we talk about bad governance, let's get everyone on the same page about what governance actually is. And just so everyone will not have to accept my word for it, I am going to a higher power. No, not the Almighty; the Organization for Economic Cooperation and Development, OECD. The reason I am going to use the OECD as our 'standard maker' is because they recognize and state it all throughout their publications, *'There is no single model of good corporate governance"* which is probably one of the reasons all the know-it-alls, all know different shit. They know what they've been taught, seen what may have worked in one organization and stick to that very narrow definition and never try to keep learning. Governance has its general purpose, like shoes. But one shoe doesn't fit every foot or specific purpose. So, one shoe doesn't fit everyone. Every company is unique, every company is special and what was built for one company cannot and should not just be copied and pasted into another. It is not sustainable. Let me put this in man speak. I can drop the engine of a Lexus into a Ferrari, and may run, for a short while. Eventually something is going to grind to a halt or cause problem after problem because the Lexus engine was not built for a Ferrari! Some stupid men thinking, "I could make it work".… I can just hear it. Dumb ass. You know that saying, the definition of insanity is repeating the same action over and over again expecting a different outcome? The most insane thing I've ever seen was a company copy and paste their own bad governance and policies into their new subsidiary, affiliate or joint ventures over and over again – and each subsequently suffering for years and years of problematic HR, operations, safety, *issue after issue after issue*. I wish I could just ask them what the hell they are thinking. Get a fucking clue! If it doesn't work for the first one, don't do the same shit for the next six projects! Completely avoidable problems if they would only have gotten the right governance in from the start.

The OECD (2004) defines 'corporate governance' as "the system by which business are directed and controlled. The corporate governance structures specifies the distribution of rights and responsibilities among different participants in the corporation such as the board, managers, shareholders and other stakeholders and spell out the rules *and procedures* for making decisions on corporate affairs by doing this, it also provides the structure through which the company objectives are set and the means of attaining these objectives and monitoring performance". Corporate governance is concerned with the basic nature, purpose, integrity and identity of a company with a primary focus on its operational sustainability and legal aspects. Governance involves defining power and limits to authority, monitoring and overseeing strategic directions, socioeconomic and cultural content externalities and constituencies of the institutions.

In the easiest terms possible, there is a separation between the owners of a company (shareholders) and the management who act on their behalf and the people actually involved in the daily grind of operations. This separation means the owners lose the ability to control every aspect of the managerial decisions. The management cannot do all of the jobs themselves and they cannot watch every employee 24/7. Mom and Dad are not home all of the time! The objective of corporate governance is to attempt to align managerial incentives with those of stakeholders. This is to control the inclination of selfishness by managerial employees, especially the C-Suite and executive management, to ensure that delegated decisions making powers are not abused to the detriment of shareholders and other stakeholders. Like driving someone else's very expensive classic car. You're not going to drive it the same as you own it, because you don't fucking own it! You can't afford it! If you could, you wouldn't be an employee, you'd be a fucking shareholder on the other side of the problem trying to figure out ways to get the drivers of your car to drive it and not break it!

The most basic components of corporate governance are i) good board practices to plan, record, follow up **and oversight**, ii) control documents to define the scope and limits of management's powers and authority, iii) required transparent disclosure to the board – *real time operations reporting to allow them to make informed decisions*, and vi) well defined shareholder rights and board commitments.

Even though corporate governance can be defined in a variety of ways, generally, it involves the mechanisms by which a business enterprise is organized in a limited corporate form and is directed and controlled. It usually concerns mechanisms by which corporate management's authority and responsibilities are defined, and they are held accountable for corporate conduct and performance.

Several codes have been developed as a guide to corporate governance; however, the best guide to global corporate governance was developed by the OECD. The **OECD (2004) Principle of Corporate Governance** is as shown below;

i. The rights of shareholders: the corporate governance framework should protect shareholders rights.

ii. The equitable treatment of shareholders: the corporate governance framework should ensure the equitable treatment of all shareholders including minority and foreign shareholders. All shareholders should have the opportunity to obtain effective redress for violation of their rights.

iii. The role of stakeholders in corporate governance: the corporate governance framework should recognize the rights of stakeholders *as established by law* and encourage active cooperation between corporations and stakeholders in creating wealth, jobs and the sustainability of financially sound enterprises.

iv. Disclosure and transparency: the corporate governance framework should ensure that timely and accurate disclosure is made on all material matters regarding the corporation including the financial situation, performance, ownership and governance of the company.

v. The responsibilities of the board: the corporate governance framework should ensure the strategic guidance of the company, the effective monitoring of management by the board and the boards accountability to the company and the shareholders.

My favorite bullet is the fifth 'v' bullet! How does the board effectively monitor your company's management? Does the board simply rely on reports given to them by the management themselves? Isn't that special! Do they go to the board and tell them how many kilos of apples they picked and how good of a job they did while picking them? It's probably a power point presentation highlighting all their accomplishments, and how wonderful you're doing. Maybe mentioning a few issues that you've already resolved, but don't fuck'en tell them about the ones you haven't! And pray that they don't actually get out their own calculators and check the numbers you have in the slide! Boards who rely on management's reporting to tell them what is going on and keep them informed about the state of the company, without a compliance program's monitoring and anonymous reporting to verify and confirm the validity of those reports, are lazy ass fuck ups. You shouldn't be on a board. You're not doing your job. Admit it; you're just in it for the perks. You never actually thought there'd be hard work involved with this cushy gig did you?

When I was in middle school, my parents did not usually check my homework; I was kind of left on my own. And there was one year I nearly failed a class the first semester. My parents didn't know because I 'fixed' my report card on the way home. (*Dad, you can't ground me, I'm over 40!*) I changed it on the way home from school in Tracy Philip's kitchen with a blue ball point pen. I could change it because the report cards were hand written then (*And yes, it was a long time ago- fuck off I'm old!*), so a D or an F could easily become a B. My parents assumed I was studying. The school never asked for the report cards to be signed and returned to prove the parents saw them. The school assumed the parents would ask about the student's performance in school. The parents assumed the school would call if anything was wrong. I trusted and relied on the fact that my school wasn't going to bother to call about me. Everyone was reporting their own apples! Isn't that nice how we all trusted each other? Now that was only one report card for me, but I know lots of kids who fell through the cracks in the system because *there was no actual system of checks and balances.* The school did their part to teach and grade. The parents did their part to punish for bad grades and reward for good grades. But the two never got together and wondered if the student changing the report card somewhere in the middle! There was no monitoring system! No compliance program.

How does the board in your company hold management accountable for failing to meet expectations? Stern looks and a scolding? Have they ever actually suspended their signature authority? Threatened to? Hinted that if they didn't get their shit straight, they may have to go to bed without desert? If the company has an actual system for monitoring, then they probably have a system of levels of consequences for failing to meet goals, right? Internal Audit alone is not enough! Studies have shown that internal auditing usually only catches about 15% of illicit actions that are traceable via accounting and usually only after they've been going on for over a year. That leaves a lot of other sneaky-ass bullshit that can and does go unchecked for a long time.

Ok, so you may have shitty governance. No problem! What is the worst that could happen? There are a lot of ways poor corporate governance will impact a company. One of the major ways is that there can be the failure of a business to grow in a sustainable way. Companies that experience growth problems will try to implement different programs or changes but neglect the basics, the foundation of the business, the corporate governance. No matter what they do, the changes will sound great, look great and may even work for a short term. But if the corporate governance, the foundation is weak, it will never hold for long. How do you know what you got on your hands? How do you know if your governance is good, or fucked up? There are a number of indicators that point to a company having poor corporate governance, for example:

INDICATORS THAT YOU HAVE SHITTY GOVERNANCE:

Weak management – mentally, emotionally, spiritually or intellectually!

- The company's management is busy, constantly fighting fires. Every meeting they seem to be having is related to 'issues and problems'. They may go from one crisis to another crisis only dealing with urgent issues without having any time for proper future planning or solving the root causes of problems – which they are either carefully ignoring, hiding or don't even fucking know about because the people under them are filtering and hiding them. *Sneaky bastards.* I think it should be mandatory for all management to read or watch Shakespeare's Othello, as a cautionary tale of office politics. *Othello and* Iago, *friends who were in management together.* I've heard people in management complain and lament that they just don't have the time to think or plan a compliance program because their ass is too busy with 'issues and problems'. If that is what you're saying, then you really actually don't have time NOT to think about it. This includes legal or audit organizations where the lawyers are too busy cleaning up after management's fuckups to get any preventative measures in place. You can keep putting out fires until you burn out or go down in flames or stop the madness. Take some time and start preventing them. It's your fucking choice, but if you go down, you'll take the rest of the company with you. And sometimes to 'go down' means courtrooms and jail. Or career changes like unemployment. When you go down and end up in prison, then 'going down' takes on a whole other meaning. Don't worry, Bubba will teach you how to go down just fine.

- Financial and compliance control protocols are casual or absent. Payments for anything, even phony contracts can be put into the system and bullshit invoices paid to whomever, unchecked. For listed companies this can result in suspension of shares trading or investigations, etc. For any company, this can mean audit items – provided the General Auditor is awake, has the quality of staff needed to do the job and the balls to fight. Special note to boards; back up your compliance officers and general auditors. They are your eyes and ears. They are at war every fucking day and if you leave them out there to watch your company's interests on their own – the good ones will leave you and then you'll have to deal with pussies that cave to management and then you're blind. Think about this! Have your shares been going down? Have they been suspended lately???? Hmmm??? A lot of FCPA fines and sentences have been made based solely on poor accounting practices. Checks and balances people... no one; I mean no one is supposed to monitor themselves. I still get a nauseous giggle every time I remember one executive saying, "Oh we have compliance. Every organization does its own compliance." What a fuck up!

• The Board of Directors and the management (*or both*) do not have the financial, analytical or compliance skills required to make informed decisions. And worse than that, they think they do but they really, really, REALLY DON'T. It's should not be a reward or privilege to be a board member. It's a fucking job. It's a very involved and heavy responsibility! If the Shareholders fail to take the time to make sure the board members and management team is fully qualified (this means actual job descriptions, minimum qualification requirements, etc.) and meets the requirements, then you're gonna get shit directors and fucked up management. Note to shareholders: get tough on board and management selection. These people literally have their hands down your pants and your balls are in one of their hands and your wallet is in the other. Don't you think that merits careful due diligence in selecting the right, qualified people?

Sometimes, even when the accounting systems generate accurate reporting, you'll face problems if the board or management does not have the skills or knowledge to appreciate or comprehend the nature of what is being forecast or reported. What do the numbers actually mean! They won't be able recognize when someone is bullshitting their way through an accountability report, if the KPI's are meaningful or just crap that can't really be measured, if the numbers and percentages have been skewed by either irredeemably dishonest or sensationally dimwitted people. Or if those are the actual numbers, what do you do with them? How do you make the lines go the other direction? Yup! *Ya'll we done got the short-bus of directors here!* They are like the emperor in the story of "The Emperor's New Clothes". My advice to all managers and board members is to listen. Listen to what is being said and presented to you, and don't be afraid to admit it… you need clarification. It is not your job to know it all, but it is your job to know and admit what you don't know and are not a Subject Matter Expert on. You have two ears, two eyes and one mouth. So sometimes, shut the fuck up once in a while, and just fucking listen. Listen to the people who actually have the degrees, credentials and years of experience on a specific subject – not just the job title. The actual credentials! Listen, with the intention of testing your own knowledge. You can do it quietly in your own head if that makes you feel better. No one will know. If the ones *with the credentials and / or experience* are telling you something you different than you know, or different from what management is saying is so, it may mean you or management probably don't know as much as you thought you did. It's ok. We all suffer from bouts of unjustifiable confidence and arrogance at times. Some people, more than others. Wonder bread, Pinheads, and the tent committee members included! (Inside joke.)

I got my driver's license in my late teens. I was so proud of myself and I was sure I looked like a hot Bond girl in my little, white Toyota. And when that car full of cute guys was honking and following me down the street, it was confirmed! I was *thexy*! Pulling up at the light, they kept motioning me to roll down my window to talk with me, but I resisted because I was playing hard to get. I was out of their league! Finally I rolled down the window, and told them I was flattered but not interested. They looked confused. But then proceeded to tell me my head lights weren't on, and it was after dark. Ok.. A dumbass moment for me to be sure and a huge reality check. I may have just passed my driver's test and have a car, but that didn't make me an experience driver, it made me a new driver. The lights came on in my teenage head to; 'Oh! So that is why it was getting hard to see!' So, don't feel bad about not knowing something that isn't your field or your area of expertise, or new to you. It is no slight on you unless a new license or job title qualifies you as the most qualified expert the moment you have it. You aren't supposed to know it all. The best managers aren't the ones who know it all, or unconvincingly act like they do. The best managers are the ones who *know they don't know it all*, and know how to source and utilize their talent in the organization of someone who does. Engaging the people and talent around them, that is what makes a great manager. You'd be surprised how much better many heads are than one. Steve Jobs quote, "*It doesn't make sense to hire smart people and tell them what to do. We hire smart people so they can tell us what to do.*"

- The board or management is controlled by one person or a small clique of members – either by fear or other means. They may ignore advice, may not delegate as required and may push through their own plans without impartial consideration of the pros and cons of those plans. Likewise when your management is led around by someone who not only can make unchallenged decisions in their area, but also has the ability to make or has undue influence over decisions unilaterally across the enterprise without any proper checks and balances – and worse, the silent masses of sheep never speaking up to cry foul! The governance should be set up to prevent or deter bullies and sneaks.

- The structure and accountability of the board becomes blurred, so executive decisions in the management are made without proper examination and review. Organizations get shuffled around, roles and responsibilities of one function get jumped into another, major change management gets implemented all without Board knowledge, review or approval. And the board just senselessly accepts these matters as information items without putting their foot down – they fail to ask the right questions, assert their authority or even get aggressive when needed. Kinda like letting hormonal teens have boy-girl sleep overs in the basement with the liquor cabinet unlocked and no supervision – cause they don't think their kids or their kids' friends are going to make any bad decisions. Fuck ups.

Inadequate compliance and accounting systems

- The management team does not have a clear picture of how the business is performing because they do not have access to the right information. This means crappy accountability reporting. Safety reports or project reports without money factored in, are useless and not worth the paper they are printed on. Also, who signed them? Is there a signature on these reports? No? Then you have no accountability measures. All reports presented to the management, board or shareholders should have the signature of the authority who confirmed they have complete confidence in the information contained in that documents! So much confidence that they put their signature on them! No signature? No confidence. No accountability. Scary bull shit, right?

Note to shareholders and boards: Watch the expressions on your management's face when you tell them from now on, any and all reports presented to the boards or shareholders must bear the signature of the executive who approves them. Watch them shit their pants a little! You'll be surprised how much they don't want to do that, and then you'll have to ask yourselves why are they so worried about putting their signatures?

Meaningless KPIs being reported on, management focusing more on the format of what is being presented rather than if what is being presented is a well thought out, measurable KPI based on the reporting organizations actual fucking charter or role in the company. If the only comments coming back are about color and form, not content, it makes me wonder if the management actually understands KPIs to begin with.

- There is limited or non-existent forecasting (this includes profit and loss) and cash flow planning, which means that management are not able to plan for possible shortfalls in cash. Try this little exercise; chart out your organization's planned vs. actual expenses for each cost center / organization for each quarter for the last five years. See a little pattern forming? Is the planned vs. actual anywhere near each other? Are the little lines all over the fucking place or do they just seem to be like a pair of ice skaters, constantly parallel and never coming close to meeting in the middle? Are they skating farther away from each quarter or closer together?

Flawed policies

- What I call 'bandaid' policies are written and put into place to address, or as management thinks for the moment 'solve a problem'. They don't jive with existing policies; there is no long term thought process. They aren't actually trained on. It is an attempt at a quick fix which puts a bandaid on what is more than likely a much deeper issue.

The "next big project"

- Normal business operations get side-lined because management is focusing on the next BIG thing in the company – a merger, an upcoming IPO, the new acquisition, joint venture, subsidiary, expansion project, etc. The full attention is on the big, shiny new project while neglecting the other daily operations.

Not 'actually' adapting to change

- Managing change and adapting to it are two entirely different things. It is one of the most significant challenges that businesses face today. You can manage the process, and still fail to adapt to the changes you actually intentionally just made. That leads companies, management and employees to fall back into old habits and just right back into the rut they worked so hard to get out of. Catastrophic consequences will result when companies fail adapt, whether those changes are driven by competition, political, economic or any other driving force. I read an brilliant article called "Culture eats strategy for breakfast," by the late business management guru Peter Drucker. I highly recommend it to any management team think of engaging in change management or structure change to their organization as a way of changing your corporate culture.

18

Is the machine working?

A. HR Turnover

This is not, *or should not* be, new information. It's normal to lose people *to a point*. But when they are running out the door, your company is bleeding brain power. That is a problem. Attrition Studies can help, but only if you do the damn thing right.

The attrition formula is easy and should not be confused with a manpower study formula. Manpower studies are to analyze numbers, recruiting strategies, budgets, turn over, etc. Attrition studies are done when you're bleeding employees and they are ready to jump out the windows and slam your company and management on social media on their way out. Attrition studies are meant to find out what is driving the rats off the ship when management isn't really even aware that the ship is sinking. I went over this earlier, but let me reiterate. How many people on January 1 (minus) how many people left = the % of your attrition rate. Now if you want to lie, or skew the numbers you'll pick which 'groups' to include in your attrition study. Regular hires and every other employee who was holding a slot in your man-power plan who left before the time they were supposed to should be included. If their body was in the building, under any employment status and they left before they were expected to – they should be included in the numbers. That includes supplemental man power, seconded manpower, consultants and contractors who left before their contract was up.

Exit surveys are a good way to get down to the 'why' people leave. They have to be reasonably short with at least some details to narrow down the reason employees are bailing out on you. Is it money? Is it your policies? Is it your management, benefits package, etc.? The survey has to be ANONYMOUS so that they can feel comfortable to tell the truth. You will have to do a quarterly analysis of the Exit Surveys to give you an idea of the reasons why people are leaving and a solution on how to resolve it. DON'T JUST REPORT STATISTICS. That is meaningless and a pussy way out of facing the ugly truths about why people are leaving your company. Remember people join companies, but they leave management. Numbers are nice; even better if they are real and not 'massaged' to hide the fact that your attrition rate is more like 30% and not 5% from the Board.

Talented, quality employees seek a healthy work environment in a solid company that will give them what they want. **CEB's Quarterly Global Labor Market**[6] organization identifies the top five things employees look for when seeking a new job are:

1. Stability
2. Compensation
3. Respect
4. Benefits
5. Work-Life Balance

Stability: Employees want to know their job is stable, some supervisor or manager can't fuck around with their livelihood and hurt their family on a whim or as a result of their own ineptitude (manager's not the employees). It has been known to happen that qualified and experienced employees butt heads with fuck up management who is less qualified. They want to know that the company gives them some protection and safety nets to protect them from stupid assholes that out-rank them. They want the security of knowing they have a good future with the company. Guess what! EVERYONE ON EVERY LEVEL WANTS THE SAME THING! *Who'd a thunk it?!* Management needs to always remember this; 'want for your subordinates what you want for yourself – even if you don't particularly like their personality or style, and you'll be a decent manager.' This

---

[6]   Latest Report Available at: http://img.en25.com/Web/CEB/CLC0712414SYN.pdf

doesn't happen if a company can't show an employee they have a chance for advancement or if the company is misusing some employees as contractors or supplemental manpower for more than the legal limit. To become a 'regular hire' for the actual level of work and fair salary for the job their actually been doing is the goal of many people. Stability allows people (that's what employees are, actual live people) focus on the work and not HR issues.

Compensation: Everyone wants to be paid a fair wage for the job you are actually doing; a fair waged not based on your name, religion, nationality, race or gender. Fair wages and benefits! A lot of companies in the region use employees for job that are far above their grade codes or salary range and never adjust their contract or wage. Again, management should want for the employees what they would want for themselves. I don't understand why human beings are so stupid on this point. They get the concept with animals but not with other people. If you want a race horse to win, you take care of them. You feed them well; invest in training, medical care, good living conditions, etc. You do all of this because you want the horse to perform well. Yet with people they act fucking retarded; they do all they can to keep salaries low, benefits out of reach, and leave their employees to have to fight for every single legal and human right they have. Then they complain that employees don't want to work and they're leaving the company. No Mr. Fuck up! The employees don't leave the company. They leave you! They leave because you're a cheap ass, lying, dirty muther who works harder to pinch them than to do right by them. Yes, I am a little bitter having seen so many good people get stepped on by so many unscrupulous managers. Sometimes management will quickly be willing to dump a lot of financial resources to cover their own mistakes, and failures at controlling contract and procurement – supply chain management, but when it comes to raising salaries and benefits for their human resources, then the budget is really restrictive.

Respect: This is directly related to what a compliance program can do for any company. Showing employees that they are respected and valued to the extent that the management has implemented a program to give them a voice, protect them from retaliation, and the rules apply to everyone at every level. This is becoming more important to people who take their career seriously and want acknowledgement. People want to know they matter, and they can make a difference. Employers demand respect from their employees and the consequences for employees failing to do their duties and give respect is termination. Employees also need respect from employers in order to remain engaged and thrive. Telling your subordinates things like, "Don't think! Just do what I tell you!" or "You don't make enough to have an opinion!" You know it may feel good and powerful to talk to people like that. But you have to know! You don't look good and powerful. You just look like an asshole. People will concede to your authority for the moment. But what they are thinking is, *"What a prick! I bet he has a really, really small penis."* The employees you demean and insult today are the very same ones who are going to race to turn you in for doing something wrong; the same ones who will set you up with a happy heart. Human beings have a limit, and paybacks are a bitch. So for those in management who say, "I don't care what they think!" I hope you're bullet proof, angel! Cause if there is anything wrong with your behavior or operations under your watch, the same people you disrespect and screw over will find those weaknesses and get you back. You'll never see it coming. People, who get disrespected and stepped on too long and too hard, become pirates. Not always the good kind of pirates. I was aware of one individual who had been bad mouthing me to my supervisor, a new supervisor who was supposed to be objective and take the time to get to know their subordinates and judge them by their own merits. I was gossiped about and it did actually harm my relationship with my new boss. About two months later, some employees posted actual events and comments made by that gossiping, micro-peter individual. And they cried foul so damn loud! "That is slander! That is defamation of character!" Here is the ironic part; what was posted (and no, it wasn't me – I don't Tweet) were actual true events. But this same person had deliberately defamed me to my new boss. What was disappointing was that the new boss actually engaged in gossip, but what do you expect from wonder-bread. He warned that I was "pushing an agenda" in the company. I was. It was an anti-corruption program. I made no secret to it. I discussed it at length prior to even arriving. Apparently, that was scary to him. So he wanted to make sure I didn't get the chance to accomplish that. I will tell you what happened on that later... in the last chapter – **New Frontiers**!

Benefits: Health benefits, housing, retirement, home ownership programs, etc. If you don't take care of your employees, they aren't going to be focused on taking care of your business. Employees who are having issues with their benefits aren't focusing on the work you hired them for. If they have to 'work' to get their HR issues resolved, then your HR isn't working. **Work-Life Balance:** Some people may live to work, but most people have a life outside of the office as well. This doesn't mean most people don't want to be committed to their jobs; only that they want a balance that allows them to be dedicated to their jobs, but dedicated to their family more. If the work hours, locations or conditions become such that your employees cannot manage any kind of life outside of the office with family, friends, continued studies, recreation and relaxation, they can and do burn out! They will burn out on you.

It is strange, that companies seem to have a genuine desire to attract and hire the best employees, but they drop the ball when it comes to keeping them. They brag about hiring the best and the brightest and treat them like they're idiots who couldn't possibly figure out shit for themselves. Stupid, shortsighted management will say, "Everyone is replaceable!" And you know what, not everyone is, except the idiot who says 'everyone is replaceable' because they obviously don't recognize the human resources they actually have. If all employees are replaceable, then they must all be equal in value. If all employees are equal, then at the end of the year, everyone should get the same raise across the company. No need to bother with performance management any more. No need to evaluate and you cannot fire anyone for non-performance because everyone is equal. BUT, what if employees aren't all equal and some outperform others? What if some employees add more value to the company? What if some are actually – special? Maybe some are harder to replace. Maybe some are worth trying to keep. Is everyone so easily replaced? Absolutely not; when productive and experience employees leave, the company feels it. In the end, manpower is not a numbers game; it's about quality not quantity! And anyone who doesn't understand that shouldn't be in management. It comes down to two well-known adages, *"You get what you pay for"*…. and, *"You never appreciate what you have, until it's gone"*. Unless you're a fuck up and just never learn.

One of my favorite anecdotes shows the responsibility management carries in regards to their organizations. Two managers were packing their briefcases after a meeting; Manager A turns to Manage B, *"Wow! I was so impressed with everything you and your people have accomplished this year! Its' amazing! You have a really great team!"*

Manager B, *"Yes! Thank you! I really have real dedicated talent working under me."*

Manager A, *"You're lucky! I haven't got anything but dead wood on my team. Just dead wood!"*

Manager B, pauses reflectively and then asks, *"Let me ask you this. If they are all dead wood, did you hire them dead or did you kill them yourself?"*

B. BUDGET VARIATIONS

Every month, every organization in a company turns in their monthly budgets and accrual forms. Every month these numbers are entered into the company's accounting ledger system and added into a report. It is routine activity and also one of the most over looked risk management opportunities. Let me tell you how. Costs are assigned to a cost center. A number. Every year the budget for each cost center is planned and approved. Every month there are expenses assigned to those cost centers. And each quarter there is a very generalized report for planned and actual report. What is really very interesting is when you prepare a report, a graph, for each cost center literally mapping out the planned (blue lines) and the actuals (red lines). This should be a five year, on-going report showing each and every quarter in the year. One year = four points on the graph. What you'll see is areas of spending which are far out of where they should be on a regular basis. Most companies will see manpower, training and other HR related cost centers very nearly right on track from the planned numbers. But you may see areas of spending that the actual is so fucking far above the planned, on a regular basis, your eyebrows will pop off your head. Areas to watch are for project spending, personal expenses (I once did one of these analyses and found the VP's jet catering expenses were routinely in excess of 2,000% over budget. No shit!) Cost centers related to services and material supplies. Routine operations cost centers which are consistently running over budget could be either a sign of bad planning and budgeting, or a number of 'unexpected' expenses – like change orders on contracts, new contracts, licensing contracts for software that was supposed to have been replace and no longer in use, termed contracts which the third party is still sending invoices for but since no one is watching or administering the contract efficiently the term date is overlooked and companies just keep right on paying. There are so many possibilities of causes – you'll only know to look and dig deeper for explanations if you are looking at the long term budget / financial activity for each cost center individually.

How are these things over looked??? Many times finance gets into such a routine mode of carrying out their financial operations and reporting, that they focus on the month by month, or quarter by quarter. When this happens, each month the overspending can be signed off on, or justified and explained away. But usually when they go to the quarterly or annual reports, they are not usually looking as closely at the individual cost center's spending behaviors. They don't usually feel the need to under normal operations because the month to month details are usually already 'done'. But that is the catch! Illicit or careless behavior hides in the open by disguising itself as 'normal operations'.

If any money is being syphoned from the company, it will appear to be in the normal operations. Watch for things like 'Routine Maintenance' cost centers which routinely exceed their budgets. You may have either really sucky planners or some third parties whose extra charges and change orders or over charges are being seen and recorded as normal expenses.

C. SILENT HOTLINE

A silent hotline is not a good hotline. There is an actual set of benchmarks for your hotline. Of all the reports you will receive, at least 85% of them should be actionable. So what is the average number of hotline reports your company should have? Don't take my word for this! A great company to access information and statistics on reporting hotlines is Navex Global.

According to Navex Global, the median number for hotline reports should be about 1.4%. If you're hotline is significantly lower, you've got a silent hotline and no trust in your company's compliance program's effectiveness. If it is significantly higher, you got other issues. Anything above .5% is a significant variation. So how do you figure out your company's average?

Take the total number of reports (R) from all reporting channels (incident reports, allegations and specific policy inquiry questions) received during the period, divide that number by the number of employees (E) in your organization.

$$(R / E) = \text{your average}$$

Navex reported that in 2010, the median average was 0.09. In 2011 it went up to 1.1, 2012 and 2013 it leveled out at 1.2. In 2014 it rose to 1.3, but in Navex's Hotline Benchmark Report for 2015, it goes up to 1.4.

Examples

# Reports Annually	# of Employees	Your %
2	100	2.00
25	3,000	0.83
50	50,000	0.10

If your % is below the norm, people are not using your hotline. Or you could just be a perfectly wonderful place to work and everyone is so happy. Pink fluffy unicorns dance on rainbows outside your offices and all is good and pure in the universe.

D. CONTRACTING

Contracting and procurement issues will run a company into trouble from every direction. From bribery, corrupted bidding practices, sloppy vetting and due diligence, project and materials delays, manpower issues, legal problems, etc. the list is huge! There are always risks involved in signing contracts, but no business can get out of it. It is the nature of the beast! Doing business requires contractual relationships; relationships with other entities that you have little or no control over. Imagine hiring a contractor to come in and do remodeling in your house, but you're not going to be home. Your kids are. Those contractors have full access to your house, and your family. Are you going to be paying attention or find ways to monitor? Of course you would, unless you're a fuck up. Contracting activity in your company should be one of the most monitored and watched processes in your operations. To make sure it goes smoothly and cleanly.

In addition to regulations and company policies, there are other relevant factors throughout contracting and procurement cycles; bidding, selecting, negotiating, contracting, administering your contracts and closing your contractual relations. All of these factors means one consistent thing, there are a lot of people involved in every step. In order to manage your risks, you need to make sure your contracting policies are completely compliant with regulatory requirements. In order to make sure EVEYONE involved in the contracting processes has the same understanding and interpretation of the policies, there must be step by step procedures. Compliance and control measures should be built into each step. One company's Contract & Procurement policies and procedures do not necessarily work for another. Every company is different. The policy and procedures need to be carefully drafted for YOUR COMPANY, sent for legal, financial, compliance and audit review.

The approach any company adopts, the resources devoted and the effort required in relation to each of the contracting steps and factors should be determined by the size, complexity, nature and risks of the entity's contracting environment and each individual contract. Some simple questions to help you figure out if you're company is on-top of things or not.

- Can you, at any given moment get a report of how many live contracts each organization is administering?
- Does that report indicate the start and expected term date of the contract?
- Does that report indicate the total value of that contract and the total amount paid to date?
- Does your company categorize contracts by value (non-prime, sub-prime and prime) in order to determine the level of approval needed? This is to ensure that contracting process doesn't get bottle necked.
- Is there a current contract & procurement policy with detailed procedures *that has been updated within the last year*?
- Do you have a sign off process for vendor/suppliers/service providers' contracts that someone *verifies by signature* (and is held accountable

for) that the services or supplies have been delivered and completed BEFORE final payment is made? This is for accountability purposes.

- Do you have a grading system for your approved vendors/suppliers? Based on previous performances – timing, budget, quality of service, etc.
- Does your third party due diligence report include compliance and regulatory reviews?
- Are you tracking and reporting, on a quarterly basis, the planned vs. actual spending for all of your contracts and agreements? Each organization should be doing this for every single contract and agreement they are administering! This should be included in each organization's annual Accountability Report's KPIs.
- Do all of your third parties / contracted parties with your company have a copy of and sign an acknowledgement to your Supplier's Code of Conduct before they are vetted as approved for your company?

This list is not all inclusive! But if you answered 'No' to even one of these questions, you got problems.

Managing risk is an essential part of good contracting. This ain't your money you're spending! It belongs to someone else – the shareholders. Take as much care of how you spend on their behalf as you would expect someone to take care with YOUR hard earned money.

The risk management, like the bullets listed above should be integrated to all aspects of contracting and procurement, including the development and management of contracts. This requires the identification of risks and this is where you literally map out the contract and procurement processes; identify necessary steps, eliminate redundant steps, ensure everything stays in line with the company's signature authority and relevant laws, identify areas where there could be risks. For example, where in the process would bribery most likely take place? During this part of the process, what check and balances and controls can you put into place to reduce or eliminate the vulnerable processes and how would you monitor this? This is an over simplification, but to tell the truth, this subject is an entire book by itself.

This mapping of the processes involves identifying the stages where risks are likely to be the highest and/or the adverse effect of an event or occurrence is likely to be the greatest. Then building in the controls, checks and balances and monitoring system, essentially 'the treatments' to manage that stage's risks. Treatments may be effected throughout the contract process.

Completing the contract is only part of the issue. Contract management and administration, this is about managing your business relationships.

Is your contracting and procurement working? Answer these questions:

- Have you had any contract disputes with suppliers?
- Has your company had any allegations or issues of bribery or unfair contracting awards?
- Has any project or business relationship suffered from legal problems of your contracted third parties? (They had criminal allegations or investigations, manpower or materials issues which slowed or stopped your project, or they failed to provide the materials or services to the standards agreed upon.)
- Does your contracting and procurement policy and procedures include Financial, technical and compliance due diligence with different levels?
- Do you have contracting templates that have undergone legal and compliance review ANNUALLY and does your contract and procurement team STICK to the template?
- Has your legal team done any training for contracting? How well do your legal and contracting organizations work together?

You should have a really good idea of what I am talking about as indicators.

E. BAD PRESS AND NEGATIVE WORD OF MOUTH

You don't really need me to explain that if your company has made the news more than once in a year's time for something bad; you have issues. Do you? Public image of your company is important. I mean it's really important! The best and the brightest employees you want to hire Google shit nowadays. They will Google the best and worst lists of places to work. They will Google salaries, benefits, reviews from your former employees, blogs, business magazines, etc. And every bit of bad press about your company will be popping upright along with it. When they're done there, they'll start looking for other people in social media sites like Linked In and Facebook. Then that brings up the other kind of bad press, the kind of 'sharing' of opinions or personal stories like 'my sister's cousin's first husband was actually there when it happened, kind of personal story. Or worse, someone who actually, verifiably did work for the company or still does is sharing horror stories. I am not talking about sharing company's confidential information; I am talking about their own personal '*that manager crapped all over my life*' or '*HR is starving my family*' kind of stories. Now let's be really, really clear here. There is a big, big difference between discussing shop outside of the shop and complaining about your own personal woes or listening to others' stories.

Employees have the right to vent, and complain. It is their right. They do not have the right to expose company confidential information to defame or slander the company by lying. But if a former employee is in the mood for sharing, no court in the world is going to allow a charge of defamation stand against a former employee who has been mistreated by a non-compliant company. Now sometimes, if you happen to be the supervisor, manager or VP or even C-Suite executive who is crapping on people or making the decisions which results in people suffering, then I can appreciate the fact that employees' complaints is not music to your ears. But keep this clear in your mind - complaining about their personnel issues is not the same as divulging company confidential information or defamation of character or slander. If one employee is complaining about their issues, it's probably not a systemic problem. If two or three are, and they are saying the same shit, listen up and start asking questions because where there is smoke, there is fire. If you have a group of employees who ask for group meetings with management to discuss problems, then don't be a fuck up! Fix it fast, because these are not YOUR employees. You may management them. You may supervise them, but they work for the shareholder. They are the shareholders' employees. And what is in their best interest is in the best interest of your shareholders. And if you're shitting where your shareholders eat, you're eventually going to be called into account. *Karma is a mean ass bitch and every fucker eventually gets their comeuppance.* Employees, who get tired of waiting for that to happen to nasty management, will take steps to hurry that up because they want to see a fucker get what he deserves as well. Employees can retaliate against management in many forms – including wicked rants on social media, personal attacks, telling the wife about the mistress, rumors, or just telling your secret shit to the world. The message here is to take care of your workforce, and they will take care of you. Don't fuck them over, they outnumber you. For complete training on this concept, watch **A Bug's Life** (1998), an American film by Pixar Animation Studios and distributed by Walt Disney Pictures. *Hint: the grasshoppers are the Management.*

Consider that for every individual who is brave enough to voice their opinions, there are most likely a dozen or two more that are silent. If you have a whole slew of people complaining about the same crap around the company on all sorts of issues, you better fucking pay attention. You got problems. If you're on a Board or in executive management and these events start to happen and it surprises you, it's your own fault; because you weren't monitoring. You were not asking the right questions. I ardently recommend an annual anonymous survey for the entire company. It can be painful to get the responses back, especially regarding employee morale. But it is an annual checkup or cancer screening. Non-compliance and poor ethics are a cancer. Bad management is cancer. The results should go to the board and the management. No filtering.

19

You've Been Served!

A. IT WILL HURT WORSE IF YOU STRUGGLE.
(Cooperate! Don't clench!)

Weatherford, in which the company agreed to pay $250 million to settle claims with the SEC and the DOJ for failure to establish internal controls and to prevent FCPA violations relating to the United Nation's Oil for Food program. Representatives from the SEC and DOJ have repeatedly made statements in the media that that they were focusing on a wide range of non-traditional FCPA violations, such as corrupt payments relating to improper gifts and entertainment, payments to avoid taxes and required customs payment and charitable donations that ultimately benefit a government official.

I would like to use the FCPA case against Total S.A. as a good example of what not to do when served!

In the fourth largest FCPA payment of all time Total SA paid criminal and civil fines in 2013 of $398 million to settle U.S. FCPA for bribing an Iranian government official to gain access to oil and gas fields. That is the "Islamic Republic of Iran" … and last I heard, taking bribes was not allowed in Islam. It makes me wonder what penalty the guy who took the bribe actually got. He was named in the court documents; the Chairman of an Iranian engineering company, in which the Iranian government owns 90% of the company. He was the head of the government organization which regulates and delegates resources related to industries which require fuel supply and consumption.

I wonder if Iran handles its corruption cases like Saudi handles it. It doesn't. The charges against Total weren't just for paying a bribe. They also got into trouble for failing to implement sufficient anti-bribery compliance procedures and policies. They failed to maintain an adequate system for the selection and approval of consultants – otherwise known as a proper third party due diligence, services and material supply chain management. They failed to implement routine audits to ensure that all payments to contractors, consultants, and service providers were for services actually rendered. They didn't have an actual compliance office or compliance program. Basically, they ran their contracting and procurement processes with the same level of self-control as a teenage boy on prom night.

Case precedent is always very important to pay very close attention to. Because there is nothing new under the sun and so many companies engage in the same bad practices. By paying attention to what other companies are getting their asses kicked for, you may be better prepared to tweak and massage your own company's compliance program policies and training to avoid the same problems. I know a lot of companies all over the world who are 'guilty' of exactly the same things, and still don't take the necessary precautions to mitigate their own risks.

Remember those old movies about the American Revolution and how the British Redcoats would stand in nice neat lines in front of the American rebel soldiers. They shout, Ready! Aim! Fire! And then they would just stand there and shoot each other. No one ducked. No one hid behind a tree or a boulder. Stupid! It was suicidal! We could see that and we were just kids when those movies came out. There was no heroics to just stand there and get shot. But there was a time when that was how it was done. And you know those soldiers had to have been entertaining the hope that it wouldn't happen to them. That they would be lucky and not get hit. Well, eventually the rebels figured it out. If the guys to your left were getting hit, and the guys to your right and in front were all getting whacked, you put pretty good odds that you only hadn't because of luck. Not skill. So eventually the rebels decided to mitigate their risks and hide.

Well the same consideration should be taken when considering companies facing criminal and civil corruption charges. If more than a few other companies are getting hit for the same types of practices you know are going on your company, you may want to start mitigating your risks. Take cover.

If the US Department of Justice and the US Security Exchange Commission consider those things worthy of a USD $398-million-dollar settlement and your organization has behaved similarly, then your risk is pretty fucking high. Remember! It wasn't just a bribery charge that got them into trouble! There are so many other things listed there and only one of them was the bribe. A lot of companies would not pass this standard and if you are one of them, you could get fucked right up ass from law enforcement. Then again, maybe that is how you like it.

Count 1: 18 U.S.C. 371. *Conspiracy to Violate of the Anti-Bribery Provisions of the Foreign Corrupt Practices Act.*

That means they had to think about it, plan it, communicate with the named parties to do it. It doesn't mean they had to succeed in any plan, only that they had a plan. How would the US know what the Chairman of an Iranian company and management of a French company were talking about on the phone, in their private emails and private meetings in Iran? Hmmm? You ever get the feeling that someone is watching and listening to you at your most vulnerable moments? *cough* NSA *cough*

Count 2: 15 U.S.C. 78 m(b)(2)(A), 78m (b)(5), and 78ff(a): Violation of the Books and Records Provisions of the Foreign Corrupt Practices Act.

Someone *cough* NSA *cough* knew they had been engaging in shady business, and now they wanted hit them again by charging them with cooking the books. You paid a bribe and forgot to write it down???? Shame on you!

Saturday:

- 12:00 luncheon meeting with Finance. Expense it as business luncheon.

- 1:30 pm, Meet with the "Chairman". Discuss illicit payment of $5 million for oil field permissions to get through. *Note to self:* Ask him how he wants to process the payment; expense it as a consulting fee.

Counts 3: 15 U.S.C. 78m(b)(2)(B), 78m (b)(5), and 78ff(a): Violation of the Internal Controls Provisions of the Foreign Corrupt Practices Act. [7] *cough* NSA! *cough*

cough The NSA knows what you did last summer. They have pictures. *cough*

There are a lot of reasons I like to use TOTAL SA as a study case. First, I think that Total was pretty confident that their compliance measures or program in the company were great as they were; just enough to be manageable and not get in the way of their operations, but enough to check the box and say they had compliance. And I am pretty sure the company was conducting business as usual all over the world, never once thinking that the NSA or any other US government law enforcement agency was investigating and watching for over a decade. And I would even be so brave as to guess that they never would have guessed that the French government would be working with the US DOJ and SEC to bust their ass! And when they were first served, I know they contested the jurisdiction initially but finally gave in and settled.

The whole thing cost them a lot more than just the USD $398 million. It cost them a serious slap to their reputation. The company entered into a three year deferred prosecution agreement and has to pay for the independent compliance monitor, a French national or French law or accounting firm — which had to be acceptable to both the SEC and DOJ. The firm had to evaluate and monitor Total's anti-bribery policies and procedures, as well as the board of directors' and senior executives' behavior, to make sure they were committed to walk the talk and implement ad effective corporate compliance program. The monitor also had to communicate regularly with French authorities, all just adding more to the list of things Total had to pay for. Imagine how a teenager would feel if they got caught drinking or smoking weed and as part of their punishment they had to give a weekly drug test, wear an ankle monitor to track their movements, and pay for the tests and ankle monitor themselves.

After the company dealt with all of the FCPA issues, it was charged by the prosecutor of Paris (François Molins, Procureur de la République) of the

---

7   US vs. TOTAL, S.A. Criminal No. 1:13 CR 239. Available at: https://www.justice.gov/iso/opa/resources/1862013529103734480930.pdf

Tribunal de Grande Instance de Paris for violations of French laws. Remember I mentioned, the US and the French law enforcement were working together. Investigating and prosecuting corruption cases is relatively unfamiliar grounds to a lot of governments. The US DOJ and SEC are the bad asses who have the backing of the NSA to help them out. You can't run. You can't hide. And personally, that doesn't make me feel bad for any executive. I just wish more governments would pick up the phone and make the decision to work with the DOJ and SEC on establishing their own anti-corruption enforcement efforts.

The SEC and DOJ have made it clear in numerous media articles that they will consider the seriousness, duration and pervasiveness of the misconduct; the nature and size of the company; and subsequent efforts the company makes to rectify the problem and prevent it from reoccurring. The FCPA guide states that companies who self-reported, fully cooperates with the investigations and shows a real commitment to improve and implement an actual compliance program will not only reduce their fines, shorten their required monitoring periods and may also be allowed to self-monitor as opposed to being forced to bear the cost of an external monitor.

The Total case provides a list of educational opportunities for shareholders to learn from, especially when dealing with third-parties or agents.

- Be really fucking careful who you sign a contract with, and make sure the middle management isn't risking your company's money or reputation by paying bribes.
- Make sure your compliance program is real, works and you're paying attention to the reports.
- If you get served, there are a couple of things you must do:
  o Cooperate with investigations
  o Don't try to hide anything, and make it a point to show that you're not either. See the next section on Hold / Non-destruction orders.
  o If someone fucked up, don't compound the problem by trying to cover them or protect them. Do not worry about holding fuck ups accountable. Protect your company, its employees and hold the fuck ups accountable – in the most transparent way possible.
  o Manage your contracts, supply chain management very very very carefully. Cause that is where the fuck ups will take advantage.

Government law enforcement agencies have given companies and executives good reason to take proactive steps in assuring that their compliance programs are well covered, particularly when it comes to engaging third-party agents and consultants. It's no secret. Third parties, your company's contracts for services and materials have proven to be fertile ground for the fuck ups to take advantage of and for law enforcement to plow when conducting anti-corruption investigations. Prevention is always cheaper than the cure.

Don't take my word for it. See for yourself. In the NY Times, journalist P. Henning addresses this very subject in his 'White Collar Watch Column, Sept. 14, 2015 edition, "The Prospects for Pursuing Corporate Executives". Henning makes it very clear what the message from the US DOJ is regarding company's protecting or hiding their fuck ups.

> *The Justice Department wants the message to go out that federal prosecutors will be taking aim at executives over their role in corporate misconduct by issuing a new policy[8] that requires companies to identify every wrongdoer within the organization, regardless of rank, **or be considered uncooperative.***
>
> *Clearly misbehaving employees need to be thrown under the proverbial bus. Yates's memorandum states to receive cooperation credit a company must disclose "all relevant facts about individual misconduct." The question is whether this will have the effect the Justice Department wants by increasing the number of prosecutions, especially of senior managers.*

Hey Wonder bread! Take notes. If a compliance professional happened to forward you a copy of the Yates policy, don't act like they are annoying you with trivial bullshit. Pay attention because they were talking to you bonehead! I am not making this shit up! And most executives won't believe that it will happen to them until it is actually happening.

---

[8]   http://www.nytimes.com/2015/09/15/business/dealbook/theprospects-for-pursuing-corporate-executives.html?_r=0

Kind of like not wearing your seat belt! Accidents happen to other people! Not you! You don't need a seat belt. Kids are fine! They don't need to be in a car seat! You're a great driver! You can handle going over the speed limit. You're great! Until you're not. Your family is dead, you're the only one that survived, and you're paralyzed in the hospital. The teenager who was speeding in the car that hit you is dead and they tell you, your family would have survived if only they'd been wearing their seat belts and secured in a car seat. Shit happens, and sometimes it happens to decent people who just didn't see the risk or their appetite for risk was bigger than the capital they had to pay for it. All you have to do is avoid the risk, take the time to do it right. Buckle up. Compliance up. Don't fuck it up.

Shareholders! Boards! It should be clearly spelled out and repeated in your company's compliance policy that the company will fully cooperate with any government investigation and that includes handing over the names and details of any individual's involvement with illicit behavior. If that isn't a deterrent for bad behavior from your management and employees, then you're not enforcing it! And that is on you.

B. HOLD / NON-DESTRUCT ORDERS

If your company ends up either the defendant or plaintiff in a legal case, you will need to be able to find and present records and documents as requested. If someone is deleting, shredding or 'loosing' documents, even if your company wasn't guilty – you sure as fuck look guilty now. Maybe it was just one person fucking around and breaking the rules. You cannot completely control and prevent people from destroying evidence, but you need to have a way to manage issues when they come up to protect the company's liability. Just like you practice fire drills in case of a fire, you need to have a clear order and procedure for sending out Hold / Non-Destruct Orders to your employees. Have a prepared message sent out to all employees in the event of a law suit and in the course of preparing for trial, records created by company's organizations may be requested. Should any individual violate that order, they should be held individually accountable. Again, protect the company and the shareholders.

A simple message like: "The legal office is affecting a Hold/Non-Destruct Order for [affected company organizations]. Be advised, until further notice no records are to be deleted, destroyed, moved or otherwise damaged in any way. Any individual found to be destroying documents before authorized to do so, will be held responsible to the company and government authorities." Or something to that affect. A clear and decisive message that the company (shareholders) will not be held responsible nor be allowed to look guilty by the actions of some stupid fucktard who thought he or she could dump evidence. And if the evidence is actually condemning to the individual or company, the company will turn it turn the responsible individuals over to the authorities. Don't take responsibility for individuals acting badly in your company! Toss their fucktard asses straight to the authorities! You'll be surprised when you take that stance, how many few incidents of bad behavior you'll have. Again, if the government comes knocking and hears the shredding machine working, you look guilty.

C. THIN LINE BETWEEN A SMILE AND A SMIRK

Law Enforcement Attorneys don't like Corporate Attorneys. They don't like you. They think you're like whores who protect criminals. They want to hurt you and take away all your toys! It's no secret… except to some corporate attorneys.

I wanted to include this story just for the sake of including it. I have a friend who is a very successful corporate attorney. He is Wonder bread but he also a great attorney and a good person. We were discussing a certain project we were collaborating on for a compliance program. He worked for a different company than I did, but we collaborated on a number of compliance matters bouncing ideas off of each other.

He was very excited about the fact that he'd met an attorney with the DOJ. I immediately sucked my breath in a little and my heart was speeding up. He was telling me that the DOJ just dropped by to meet his legal team and it was a great and friendly visit. He took it as they just wanted to rub elbows with us cause we're so amazing an awesome kind of glee!

I cautiously told him I thought he ought to be a little concerned and I don't think the DOJ is in the habit of making social visits to foreign corporations. He literally laughed me off and tried to explain that of course everyone in the legal field would want to meet them and hang out with them because they were so frick'en awesome! I remember thinking, 'Oh man. He drank the Kool-aid."

I finally flat out told him, that was not the case. I tried to explain that law enforcement attorneys and corporate attorneys are natural enemies in the world. He didn't see why. His feeling was that they are lawyers, and we are lawyers (him not me!) and there is a professional and mutual respect and admiration.

But there really isn't. Corporate lawyers need to understand that in the eyes of law enforcement, you are as bad if not worse than mafia lawyers. Because corporations are viewed as evil and executives are seen as evil incarnate – the cause of environmental destruction, global warming, and explosions which kill children forced to work in factories, injustice done to minorities or protected classes, etc. You name it! Plus you make more money than they do, and have better toys and offices.

Corporate attorneys who defend the companies and their executives should never make the mistake of thinking that there is mutual respect. In law enforcement's mind, you are overpaid, arrogant and need to be taken down. One SEC attorney gave an interview in which he commented that while the SEC and DOJ felt good about getting those huge fines from companies for FCPA violations, what gave them more joy than anything was to successfully arrest and prosecute executives – because they are under the impression that they are bullet-proof and untouchable. It was one of those articles where you say out loud, "OH! Snap!" and then email it to your friends that are corporate attorneys with a snarky subject like, "Look! They don't like you either!" Six months later, you decide to include it in your book at the last minutes and can't find the fucking original article to cite!

Board members and management also need to keep something in mind. If the company is in trouble, the lawyers who work for the company will do their jobs and take care of the company's interest. But if you fuck up, you're not the company. When shit starts getting real, you will be sacrificed and thrown under the bus if you fuck up – to protect the interests of the company. Your law department attorney's cannot represent you in a case of corruption – they only represent the company because if you're fired, broke and in jail, you are not paying their salary.

And those trusted legal eagles in your law department are not liked by law enforcement either. Make sure they don't get cocky with law enforcement in communications if there is an investigation or case against the company. It will be like pulling the tiger by the tail, or poking the bear with a stick! And you people in management or the boards are the first ones who're gonna get bitten.

The moral of the story is, run your company clean and compliant. There may be short lived financial or other benefits to illicit behavior but the risk is not worth the reward. And never put your faith in the lawyers to save you from your own mistakes – because they can't and they won't. Corporate lawyers are not martyrs. They won't take a fall for you. They won't take a bullet for you. And if they have to protect themselves, they'll be the first ones to rat your sorry ass out.

If law enforcement knocks on the door, even if the real reason is not immediately apparent, NEVER assume it's a social visit. There is a carefully thought out reason and purpose to everything they do – just like your own lawyers, they always got a plan. Some of my best friends are corporate lawyers, but I am no fool to think they'd risk themselves or their employers / clients for any single individual. They're just not built that way.

> *"Corporations can only commit crimes through flesh-and-blood people. It's only fair that the people who are responsible for committing those crimes be held accountable," said Sally Q. Yates, the deputy attorney general.*

Note to shareholders: law enforcement is getting tougher on corruption. Protect your company and your assets by making sure your management is held accountable and lives up to your expectations of how you want them to run YOUR company and manage YOUR money.

SECTION IV

New Frontiers!

For every bad executive or manager or careless board member I've met, I've met a hundred great employees and I include some very good management among them. The differentiation being that good management stands with their employees, leading by example and not against them or on their necks. I think of great managers and supervisors as employees – because they know they know that regardless of their position of privilege and salary, they bear the responsibility for taking care of the company as a trust.

One of the best managers I had ever had the pleasure of working with told me once that he always felt a lot of pressure in his job. He said, "If I make mistakes, people can die." He went on to explain that he never felt like a 'boss', and hated to be referred to as 'boss'. He considered himself rather like a father to his organization and he meant it in a 'protective' manner not one of condescension. He just knew that his people relied upon his protection and to have their best interests at the heart of his decision making and they wouldn't follow him or work for him if they didn't trust him. He would be the first to own that he didn't know it all, but that he would listen to his subject matter experts and team for information. He remains one of the best listeners I've ever met. On the flip side, he got to where he was because the shareholders trusted his dedication to them as well. He would never betray the trust they put in him to take care of their assets. Trustworthiness, integrity was at the core of everything he did. In the 9 years I knew him, I never heard one person ever say a negative word about him. He was a great mentor to me. And as well as he tried to advise me, mentor me and help me in my career path, he could not save me from myself.

I've been living and working in the Middle East for 20 years. I am very good at my job but I don't think I am in the right field for a person with my particular mindset. The idea of corrupt management getting thrown down on the ground, handcuffed and carted off to jail makes me giggle. Management doesn't like that. I may need to rethink things.

I started out very young working with the Portland Police Bureau in Oregon, with a program called Women Strength. I taught self-defense and sexual assault prevention for girls and women 12 years old and up. I did a lot of public speaking on personal safety and prevention of crimes. Prevention is the key word here. I think it molded my mind-set to certain path that prevention is always better than the cure; a mindset that holds ideals like accountability, integrity, responsibility and transparency in very high reverence. Shit. No wonder I freak so many managers out!

I believe in prevention, lowering risk, and keeping your eyes and ears open for danger zones. I had always wanted to continue along this career path and go into law enforcement but I was also very young and made some rash decisions which took me into a whole different world. Not 'Hell' exactly, but I can see it from here. For a long time, I thought that part of me was gone; the fighter, the rebel… the pirate. My senior year history teacher Mr. Weinstein called me a rabble-rouser. But having been working as a compliance professional for the past few years I have come to realize that mindset is not gone. In fact, it's more alive and kicking than I could have imagined.

I am exhausted, embittered, disillusioned, and basically really fucking pissed off trying to convince management of corporations to follow the laws, to comply with regulations and trying 'sell' them on the idea that compliance is good for them and the company in the long run. The truth of the matter is that while it is great for companies, compliance programs are fucking risky for management. Of course they're not going to embrace them. If governments' authorities and law enforcement are really enforcing anti-corruption laws in the Middle East, it would be different. But a gross failure to hold powerful individuals in corporations accountable is worldwide problem. Even in the US!

How many Wall Street executives have been prosecuted for their part in the financial crisis that they caused?? To date, none!

If a company's management is not being required by law to implement a compliance program from a risk of prosecution stand point, and the board is doing a half-ass job of monitoring, it falls on the shareholders to insist on it. If the shareholders don't give a shit to do it, then the employees will have to make a choice – stay and tolerate it, leave and find a better employer, or sue the fuck out of the company and make the shareholders take note. *I am really getting more convinced I am not cut out for corporate life.*

Until governments make the conscious decision and commit to enforce anti-corruption laws, and really go after those individuals who are conducting bad business, the only real risk to fucked-up and corrupt management is if the shareholders or sometimes boards find out about them. The only way they find out how fucked up the management is will be if there is a compliance program in place or if there happens to be a legal action which costs them money.

I don't know why it took me so long to fully comprehend and accept the reality of this. I have been overly optimistic and delusional. You cannot sell compliance to management without the insistence of the board, shareholders or requirement of government any more than you could convince an unruly teenager to wear an ankle bracelet and take daily drug tests just because it will be better for their future. That is way too much accountability and exposure for them.

And there I was, the eternal optimist and do-gooder thinking if I could just convince them how beneficial it was and continued peddling anti-corruption compliance all over the Middle East. Got lots of meetings, but ….

When I was young, I had been accused of suffering from White Horse Syndrome, and that I would ride that white horse right over a cliff trying to save the world. I think it's better now for me to trade in the white horse for a three corner hat, and a meaner, more suspicious attitude.

At the end of the day, everyone is losing; the shareholders, the employees, and the communities / economies these corporations are supposed to be taking care of. Companies, their assets, and their employees are being so poorly managed that we will all be the losers in the long run.

Shareholders may be seeing some financial benefits in the short term, but shit always comes out in the end. There are no real secrets.

Governments are losing because corruption costs them a lot of money in the end, and when a government fails to enforce anti-corruption and punish individuals, they just look like fucktards as well.

Funny thing about secrets, in the corporate world there really aren't any. Someone always knows something they shouldn't or something that management doesn't want them to. Lots of people are so sure 'no one will ever find out' their dirty little secrets. They are confident, overly confident in their ability to keep things hidden. Well, not so.

Take the Titanic for example. Lots of people speculated on how a ship that was supposed to be unsinkable, sunk. Was the damage greater than they knew? Was it poorly built? When they began raising pieces of the Titanic the answers came up to. Even secrets lost at the bottom of the icy ocean, come up.

People have been theorizing for decades about the assassination of John Kennedy. Was there a second shooter? Did the gun of the secret service agent in the car behind Kennedy accidently discharge when the car lurched forward in all the commotion from the first shots fired? Is it possible that the Kennedy family knew and let it remain a secret because they understood it was an accident? Perhaps they allowed that knowledge to be buried to protect the agent and his family from a life time of blame and retribution. I was born in 1968, how could I have come across that theory? Conspiracy theory or a peek at what may be real… there are no secrets.

Law enforcement and shareholders: How do you get people to spill those corruption secrets and start exposing corruption more? A good place for any government to start is to establish an anonymous reporting mechanism, strong whistle-blower protection AND REWARDS! Think about this for just a minute. Remember the case against Total SA that we discussed? USD $398 million dollars! What if a whistle-blower actually got 10% of that fine? Do you know anyone that wouldn't turn in corrupt management for a cool US $39 million? Fuck yeah! Crime should pay, for whistle-blowers.

Personal note here; I don't like the term 'whistle-blower'. It makes it sound so like the dorky kid who used to tell on everyone else in the class. Like anyone who blows the whistle-blower is a tattle-tale, a narc, or some goody two shoes. They are not. They are very courageous people who stand up for their principals even at their own risk. It is one of the hardest things in the world to do. Having to make a decision to stand up and speak out, risking your career and livelihood, or accept the corruption around you. I think being so cowed and afraid of retaliation, that you have to conform to deviant behavior or at least turn a blind eye, is soul crushing. I have lost more sleep in my life from things I'd wished I'd said or done vs. the things I did or said that I shouldn't have. I think we should change the term whistle-blower to white-hat pirates; 'White-hats' for short.

But what if people were able to safely speak out and were even rewarded for doing so? What if… what if some poor guy working a shit job in some shit company has, in his hands at this very moment, a shit load of evidence that the management of his company was cheating their shareholders, risking the environment or the even the lives of its employees? What if their behavior and misconduct – criminal behavior – was undermining what laws and regulations you were trying to enforce? (I'm talking to governments in the Middle East now.. as if they'd listen!) What if you launched a white-hat protection law (and of course enforced it) as well as a 10% or 20% reward for substantiated evidence against some fuckups who were breaking your laws? If that poor guy who knew where the proverbial bodies were buried was confident that if he got that evidence to you, you would listen, start an investigation and ended up charging a company or its executives heavy fines. What if the 'trusted' the fuck-ups would be punished and go to prison and the white-hats would get a reward for it? How many people would be coming forward then?

There is a growing voice and movement of government officials who want to fight corruption but there is just so much of it, it is hard to know where to start. And no matter where you start, you'll always end up with people you actually know because the 1% are the ones who are most dirty. How committed will you be in fighting corruption if it leads you to discover friends, family and respected business associates are dirty?

If companies would use anonymous hotlines more in Saudi, Shareholders and boards would get calls and start screaming, "What the fuck just happened to our company??!!" People would be fired! News would be released in the media about the investigation and sentences and fines. And the reports would mention the case was brought to the authority's attention via an anonymous white-hat – known only to the government – who will be given 10% of the total fine.

The authorities would look good for having enforced the laws successfully. The shareholders would have a chance to improve their company and clean house – run a better business. Lives could be saved. Assets protected. People protected. A clear message would be sent out far and wide that law enforcement is no longer fucking around! And that poor guy would be set for life, secure that he would have enough money to take care of his family and go to Disney Land! No, fuck that. Universal Studios in Florida AND California! Rewarded for his courage and not retaliated against. Then all of the other poor guys working in shit job in other shit companies would start getting ideas… hmm. Remember Joe, the guy who died at the party? Someone knows where he is buried. Fuck! I'd bet for the right amount of money and the protection of anonymity someone might call the FBI and tell them where the hell Jimmy Hoffa actually ended up! Just the idea of a successful White-hat payoff would be enough to make some management start wearing their brown pants to work daily.

I personally believe corporations, commerce and industry are good. It is the individuals in organizations, just as Yates stated, flesh and blood individuals, who are the fucktards making bad decisions and engaging in illicit behavior. Yates probably doesn't know it, but she is a pirate. A proper pirate at that!

As a corporate professional, I should be driving my discussion towards selling the compliance program benefits to the management who doesn't want to put in the kinds of controls that would ultimately expose them. But I am tired of that. I am just looking to the authorities and shareholders to do the right thing. Seriously! Grow some nuts and do the right thing. On second thought, grow some ovaries. You're nuts haven't been serving you very well so far.

I am looking to governments to invest more effort to anti-corruption law enforcement. As for me, I am thinking I should revisit my first and best idea of going into law enforcement myself. Thirty years later... would it be possible? Let's fucking find out!

Yo ho! Yo ho! A pirate's life for me!

Savvy?